The
NABC
Basketball Drill Book
Volume 1

Edited by

Jerry Krause,

United States Military Academy

mp
MASTERS PRESS

A Division of Howard W. Sams & Company

Published by Masters Press
A Division of Howard W. Sams & Company
2647 Waterfront Pkwy. E. Drive, Indianapolis, IN 46214

© 1998, National Association of Basketball Coaches

98 99 00 01 02 03   10 9 8 7 6 5 4 3 2 1

Library of Congress Cataloging-in-Publication Data

The NABC basketball drill book / edited by Jerry Krause.
      p.   cm.
   Includes bibliographical references
   ISBN 1-57028-148-3 (trade)
   1. Basketball -- Training. 2. Basketball -- Coaching.   I. Krause, Jerry.
   II. National Association of Basketball Coaches of the United States.
GV885.35.N23 1998   98-12624
796.323--dc21   CIP

TABLE of CONTENTS

PART I. Offensive Fundamentals Drills 1

Stance and Steps
Pass, Catch, Ballhandle
Shoot
Rebound
Team — Transition, Zone, Man

PART II. Defensive Fundamentals Drills 83

Stance and Steps
Rebound
Team — Transition, Zone, Man

PART III. Combination Drills 119

Stance and Steps
Conditioning
Offense, Defense, Transition

"If it's going to be, it's up to me."

This book is dedicated to the basketball coaches all over the world who are always searching for that one drill that, when adapted to their situation and system, will allow them to become a better teacher and coach. Be the master of your own basketball destiny by choosing the drill(s) that helps you become a better coach.

Acknowledgements

Primary appreciation goes to the NABC Board of Directors who have long supported my efforts to give something back to the game that has been so good to me.

Special thanks to the NABC Executive Director Jim Haney and his excellent staff for their help in the project.

I also acknowledge Tom Bast of Masters Press for suggesting this companion book to **Coaching Basketball**. Thanks to Holly Kondras, my editor, for her patience in producing the manuscript. And to Chrystal and Julie for assistance in completing the project.

Credits:
Diagrams by Jeremy Adams
Cover designed by Christy Pierce and Debra Wilson
Proofread by Pat Brady
Front cover photography by Brian Spurlock

Preface

Basketball is a simple game; your team finds methods to score baskets when on offense and prevent opponents from scoring when on defense.

These dual purposes of scoring and preventing scores are always based on your team properly and quickly executing the fundamental skills of the game. A coaching educator is one who can motivate players and use appropriate DRILLS to *develop* those basic movement skills in all their players. It is hoped that basketball coaches will examine these drills critically to adapt to or adopt for their system and be useful tools for developing the basketball skills of their players.

The origins of this book came from the successful NABC *Coaching Basketball* book (also Masters Press), which was developed around the theme of championship coaches at all competitive levels of basketball: professional, college (NCAA I - II - III, NAIA, and community college), and high school. In addition, the *NABC Basketball Bulletin* was researched to find drills from Basketball Hall of Fame coaches. So it is seen that drills from championship coaches were gathered to help you as a coach. Come join these coaches to develop and improve your program.

Key to Diagrams

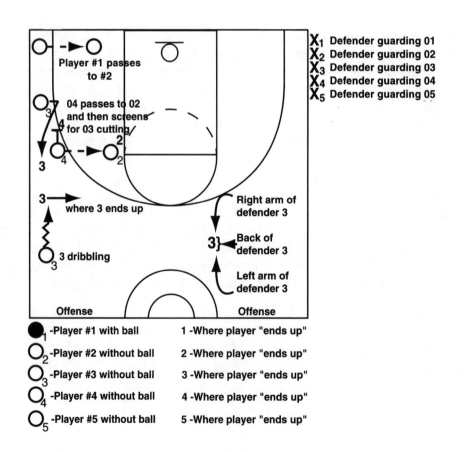

Player #1 passes to #2

04 passes to 02 and then screens for 03 cutting

where 3 ends up

3 dribbling

Offense

Offense

X₁ **Defender guarding 01**
X₂ **Defender guarding 02**
X₃ **Defender guarding 03**
X₄ **Defender guarding 04**
X₅ **Defender guarding 05**

Right arm of defender 3

Back of defender 3

Left arm of defender 3

● ₁ **-Player #1 with ball**
○ ₂ **-Player #2 without ball**
○ ₃ **-Player #3 without ball**
○ ₄ **-Player #4 without ball**
○ ₅ **-Player #5 without ball**

1 **-Where player "ends up"**
2 **-Where player "ends up"**
3 **-Where player "ends up"**
4 **-Where player "ends up"**
5 **-Where player "ends up"**

Foreword

*T*hese articles, both by coaching legends of basketball, remind us of essential
practice principles and the critical development of the role of basketball drills.
Coaches John Wooden and Tex Winter have a combined century of basketball experience.

The Daily Practice

John Wooden, Head Basketball Coach
University of California-Los Angeles
Basketball Bulletin, December 1973

It is quite probable that the success or failure of most coaches will be in *direct
proportion to their ability to devise practice drills to meet their particular needs and
then properly coordinate them into the daily practice program*. A tremendous knowledge of the game itself will be wasted, unless the ideas can be successfully taught to
the players.

It is as important for the coach to be able to teach his ideas to the players under
his supervision, as it is for the player to be able to properly *execute the fundamentals* they have been taught.

Each practice should be carefully planned and organized in order to prevent
waste of time. There must be *a specific purpose for every drill* and *every drill must
be placed in the most advantageous time during the practice period*. A drill used at
an improper time is about as useless as a drill that has no concrete purpose at all.

The daily practice program should never be planned in a hurry, but at a time
when the coach and his assistant can consider all relevant factors and then develop
the program for the day. Both the past and the future must be taken into consider-

ation as well as personnel, physical condition, morale, available facilities, and many other things.

I keep a record of all of our practice sessions from year to year and keep the record of the two previous years at finger tip for reference when planning our practice for the day. Comments are made in regard to each drill after each practice and then written at the side of the record that I keep. This serves as a very valuable reference.

Here are a few of the things that I feel I must be aware of:

1) Once the practice starts, the planned program must be followed to the letter. If not enough time was allowed for a drill, you must not continue it past the designated time. This would mean that you would either have to eliminate something else that you had felt was important or you would have to run overtime. Neither would be advisable.

It is possible to add something occasionally when you may have allowed too much time for a specific drill or you may replace a drill with another in case of the loss for the day of a specific player around whom the drill might revolve due to an injury or involuntary absence.

2) Be certain to start each practice with warm up drills that are specifically devised to loosen them up well. Stretching, bending, and jumping drills should be used as well as running and should be progressive in intensity.

3) Drills must be varied from day to day to prevent monotony, although it is possible that some will be used every day. This should be true of warm up drills just the same as shooting, rebounding, defensive or any other.

4) If the purpose of every drill is explained before it is used the first time, the players generally respond better.

5) The same drill should not be continued too long. It is better to have more drills for the same purpose.

6) Physically difficult drills should be followed by more pleasurable drills and vice-versa.

7) Drills should be as competitive as possible and should simulate game conditions whenever possible.

8) New drills should always be presented early in the practice period the first time before the players have become too tired and their learning processes slowed down. I feel that it isn't wise to try to practice a new drill the first time it is presented, but always come back with it the next day and start practicing it.

9) Every effort should be made to condition the players for game competition and the drills should be devised and used to best advantage for that purpose.

10) More time for team drills must be allowed as the season progresses, but never forget, overlook, or neglect the individual fundamentals which should always take up at least fifty percent of the practice time.

11) Analyze each day's practice while it is still fresh in your mind. I like to discuss the practice with my assistant before leaving the dressing room and make notes which will be taken into consideration when planning the practice for the next day.

12) Combine as many fundamentals as possible in many drills even though emphasis may be on one only. Do not permit a player to develop a bad habit in one fundamental merely because your emphasis is on another.

13) Use small carefully organized groups of from three to five players for teaching fundamentals. Of course, there will be times when you will have all your guards, and forwards, and post men in their own specific groups. However, you must remember and act accordingly that each player doesn't need the same amount of time on each fundamental.

14) Although it is almost impossible to work on one without the other, offense and defense should be emphasized on alternate days. The top six, seven, or eight players should be on offense during the time permitted for the development of team play on an offensive day and on defense on a defensive day.

15) Close each practice with a drill that will leave both players and coaches in a pleasant, optimistic frame of mind. This is good for everyone, including the wife and children of the coach.

Condition players before this last drill as you do not want them to leave the floor feeling punished.

BACK TO THE BASICS
Fred "Tex" Winter
Chicago Bulls
Basketball Bulletin

As coaches, we must be sold on our ideas of coaching basketball. I honestly believe that I know as much about basketball as anyone in the profession. I am a student of the game and have spent many years in developing my coaching philosophy and coaching techniques and methods. You young coaches must believe that you, too, possess a vast understanding of basketball knowledge. You possess knowledge so great that it is impossible to teach all that you know. Acquiring the knowledge requires each of us to be alert, and to concentrate on the many opportunities to learn and observe the game from the use of television, video-tape, attending clinics and seminars, visiting with fellow coaches and being creative with the situation and material at hand. Grasp those good ideas (ideas, concepts that you can understand and use) and disregard those ideas that are no value to you.

It is very important to realize that you cannot teach all the basketball that you know to be a good coach. There is not enough time available to teach all that you know; therefore, you must be selective and convey to your players are the most important parts that they should know; you the coach, must set the priorities. Furthermore, you cannot take what other coaches teach and make it yours. You must develop your own philosophy, methods and coaching style, using ideas of others where you can, but you must teach your personality because you are the only one that truly understands your own situation and circumstances. You must coach according to your particular situation. Be flexible and be able to adjust to changing situations. Each job demands unique understanding of the setting and the situation.

I. Essentials of Coaching

A. The answer to success in coaching does not lie in some form of super strategy, or some ultra super plan.

B. Success, overall, does rely on basic sound teaching abilities. The ability to teach the fundamental skills (basic basketball) to the individual athlete is critical. Your players must understand that their natural ability can take them only to a certain level.

C. Athletes must strive to break those physical barriers of endurance, speed, coordination, reflex action, jumping ability, etc., to truly become a better athlete.

D. As coaches we must develop and organize out-of-season programs that promote greater total development of our athletes, so that they can break those physical barriers.

E. Total preparation of the mental, emotional and physical aspects of athletes then, permit greater technical preparation.

F. A player has not learned a fundamental until it becomes second nature (a habit). Automatic reaction is the goal of skill execution. No thought process necessary; react.

G. Basketball is a game of total quickness, a game of reaction.

H. Athletes *are in the process of learning* and have not learned a skill until they can perform a skill correctly and quickly while involved in game situations, automatically.

I. **The coaching objective is accomplished through continuous repetition of drills and exercises.**

J. Practice does make perfect – *only* if the proper techniques and mechanics are being practiced. Proper techniques become movement habits.

K. **Repetition must be done with high levels of interest, enthusiasm and in an exciting manner until it becomes an instinctive reaction.**

L. One thing that highly disturbs me is the fact that I see so many bad habits being practiced today at all levels, from the junior high to the professionals.

M. We must demand correct execution of basic skills.

N. Design practice time and situations so that it provides the technical know-how for the individual and the team of all the phases of the game that we plan to use in the total game plan.

O. Practice sessions must be so designed to lead to superb physical conditioning. Basketball is a game that cannot be played properly unless you are in the very best possible physical condition.

P. Evaluate your practices to determine if they are designed to prepare the individual player; physically, technically, mentally and emotionally. If these factors are included then we should be able to visualize victory. (See victory in the mind's eye).

II. General Principles of Discipline and Coaching Behavior

I have always been very much concerned about the many ideas and practices of controlling or disciplining a team, and I have researched this area in great detail, and offer these findings to you.

A. I have no set rules of discipline, either for the treatment or the punishment that will be employed in particular situations.

B. Each situation will depend upon the *coach,* the *team,* and the individual(s) involved, plus the situation at hand.

C. Discipline players as individuals (different mentality, different sets of background, different experiences and different expectations). A good coach must relate and adjust to these individual differences.

D. Each disciplinary case is settled on its own merits, rather than according to pre-set rules. The player and I sit down and attempt to arrive at a solution based on what I think is best for the basketball program – not necessarily what is in the best interest of the player. I try to save the individual if I can, and they know this.

E. We have some basic practice rules.

1. Be on time for all practices.

2. Keep everybody busy learning those basic basketball skills we will use in our plan.

3. Correction of all errors will be given to assure each individual attention and success.

4. Right conduct and execution of skills is praised (motivational techniques).

5. Mistakes and errors will be pointed out and constructive criticism is given to help the player/team.

F. Criticize the act – not individual. Coaching should build rather than destroy, and all criticism is offered in a personal, one-to-one, private session, not as a squad function. Sarcasm is seldom desirable.

G. Rules are for prevention rather than for the treatment.

H. Each player is labeled either as an asset or a liability. Each decides his position by his conduct and effort.

I. By keeping practices interesting and alive, we eliminate boredom, which may be a major cause for lack of attention.

J. As coaches, we must keep our temper under control. If we expect a poised ball club, we must be poised coaches. The controlled temper is a very strong motivational force.

K. Avoid "carping" and nagging. Take corrective action, *then,* drop the matter. Don't carry a grudge, that can become a deadly diversion between and among you and your players.

L. I believe that the very best coaching and teaching is being done at the junior and senior high school level and that is where it is needed.

M. As teacher/coaches we must always consider the individual differences of age, playing level, experience, personality, emotional stability and makeup. Know the total person and remember that the younger the athlete, the more sensitive he or she will be. At the pro level you are dealing with the "over-inflated ego" and he must have that type of ego if he ever expects to make it in the pro ranks, but be aware at your of coaching. Junior high athletes are not miniature pros.

N. When dealing with individuals on a team, the team members must understand this fact, your primary concern is "what is the best for that basketball team" – with an attempt of course, to do what you can for the individual, so that each fits into the overall scheme. Try to avoid personality clashes. Do not deal in personality -personal vanity should not enter into the picture at all. Disciplinary problems will not be taken as a personal affront – revenge is not in your heart.

At the age of 36, I was a National Coach of The Year. My Kansas State team had won 25 and lost 2 and I thought I was the greatest thing since sliced bread. Today I am twice the coach I was then.

III. Practice Sessions

A. Be prepared, study past practice schedules, films, drills. Evaluate everything you plan to use this season.

B. Outline a complete yearly practice schedule.
   1. Preseason.
   2. Seasonal (Oct. 15 to tournaments).
   3. Post season.
   4. Off-season.

C. The secret of success is organization. Add what you want to add, and delete that which you want to do away with.

D. When you step on the floor, know:
   1. WHAT you are going to teach.
   2. HOW you are going to teach.
   3. WHY you are going to teach it.

   "The Six Honest Serving Men of Experience, taught me all that I know, they are: *who, what, where, why, when* and *how.*" (R. Kipling) (Know and use these six elements in developing a plan of action).

E. Daily practice.

   Two hours a day: from Oct. 15, to Nov. 1, if the gym is available. All players are on the floor one half hour early for individual practice with the assistant coaches. This time is the opportunity for the assistant coaches to teach his expertise, his special skills. Watch when the head coach comes on to the scene, the players stop paying attention to the assistant coaches; the player wants that head coach's attention.I have always had too big a team. I can't cut people, but regardless of how many we keep, everybody gets the same, equal opportunity to work. After November 1, when I start to pick the starting five, or the top ten, I have the necessary information to base my decisions on. But I truly believe I have a duty to give everyone that I invited out for the team an equal chance to make that team. All of you know that the greatest problems we have are from those players that are sitting on the sidelines who want to play and in their own minds know that they can play equally well as those out there playing.

F. We jump rope everyday (365 days a year) for speed and hand-eye coordination. I recommend that they jump twice a day for a period of five minutes, this helps to develop "quick feet." If you can't move your feet, you cannot play basketball.

G. It is important that players do some slow stretching prior to practice. It is a good idea to bring in someone that is an expert in teaching stretching exercises. Stretching helps to prevent injuries.

H. We use ball handling drills; like the Globe Trotter drills, to develop quick hands (behind head, behind back, around the torso, through the legs, etc.)

I. We want the players to thoroughly know the ball: feel, touch, smell, listen, taste the ball. Be detailed in your introduction of the ball. How much does it weigh? How big is the ball? How large is the goal? They must be totally familiar with the tools of the game. Teach relationships: little ball – big basket.

J. Take advantage of the many teaching tools and aids, such as the "toss-back" rebound machines.

K. **The use of drills, that are part of the actual game situations you plan to use are important. Don't drill just for the sake of drilling – *make drills realistic*.**

L. *Drill example*: we teach drills that include all phases of our game, such as conditioning, floor spacing, ball handling, offensive and defensive fundamentals and the like. In one of our drills, we stress running at three quarter speed and maintaining 15 to 18 feet spacing. This spacing is a critical distance in many phases of our game. The players must instinctively know that distance.

M. Basketball is a full court game "end-line-to-end-line". *Use drills that use the whole floor.* A change of speed and direction drills, pivot and sprint drills, jump and run, or anything that you plan to teach in the total game concept.

N. In closing, don't let your players practice bad habits. Demand that each practice bring the team closer to the team's goals.

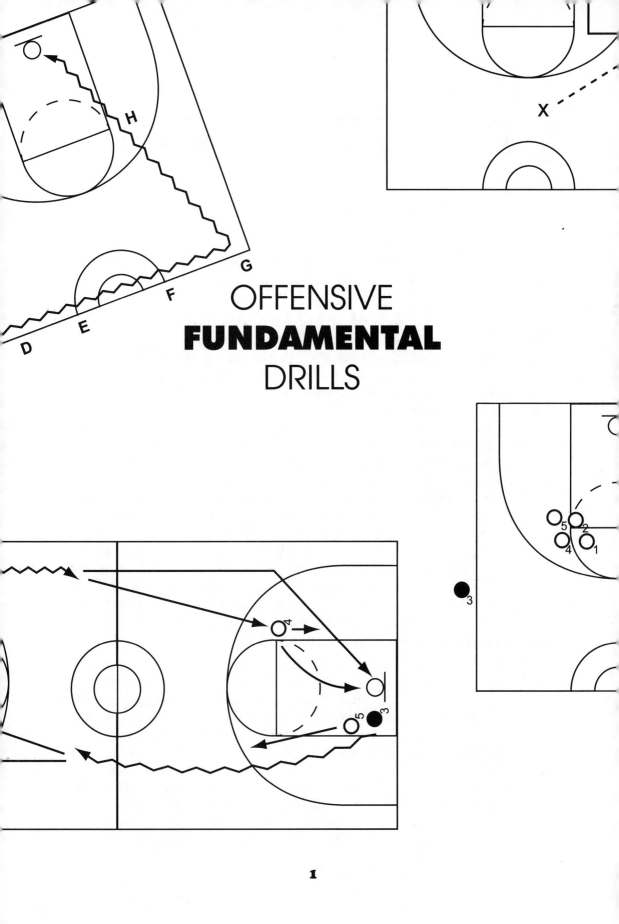

OFFENSIVE
FUNDAMENTAL
DRILLS

DRILL
1

Footwork Drills
Spring '80 Basketball Bulletin

Purpose:

Teach offensive footwork and balance as the individual fundamentals of motion for all offensive skills.

Description:

During summers I spend time teaching individual skills to basketball players. Most of these players are established NBA players and in some instances college players. It has been a labor of love in a sense for me as the players have asked me for help, and their cooperativeness, receptiveness and desire to improve has been extremely rewarding for me. I have always been stimulated by the aspect of basketball teaching to receptive people.

I believe the game should be more openly discussed between player and coach. I spend a great deal of time talking the game with these players, challenging their thinking, discussing many of the "whys" of basketball. They seem to really enjoy these cerebral sessions and, I hope, they learn from them.

The principle reason I have put this material together is to satisfy some coaches who have witnessed these practice sessions of mine with these players. I have been asked if I had any written copies, which I hadn't. These coaches feel it would be important to them to have the materials, so I have compiled it in written form.

I have taken one phase of the game — a forward one-on-one situation, as the basis for teaching footwork and balance. Obviously I taught it in more forms, but these described drills I have as part of this material are what I used to teach these individuals. I have guards and centers as well as forwards executing these moves.

THE IMPORTANCE OF TEACHING FOOTWORK

It is my opinion that there is less individual teaching of footwork, balance, variable use of individual skills and individual movement offensively than ever before. There is more coaching of a 5-man team offense and defense than ever before. We have come 180° from a game too individually oriented to a game that is now too 5-man oriented. In short, we have an overcoached and under taught game.

The skills of clever movement and good balance has been sacrificed in many coaches' minds for high jumping and physically overpowering skills. There is a tendency to emphasize the height of one's leap to the detriment of his balance and movement. The offensive movement many coaches employ stresses making the shot "off the ball" rather than "on the ball." While I will concede that the "one-on-one" concept was not and is not the answer, I don't believe the five-man motion is the total answer either. Somewhere between the two would be my thinking.

Because of the "off the ball" coaching emphasis, there is a growing lack of player skills on the ball. This referred-to emphasis has caused an erosion of the fundamentals of balance; individual footwork skills, indirection of movement drills, pivots and various turns, and creation of the shot "on the ball." Motion offense does not lend itself well to breakdown or part method teaching. The result is a minimum of coaching attention to the individual's needs of improved balance, footwork and movement.

How much time is given to individual needs in the practice plan that the coach devises for his team? What importance is given to proper movement, correct body stance while in motion, maneuvering speed, ability to stop, change direction and accelerate? Can pivots and turns be properly executed and with some knowledge of why they are being executed? Naturally the practice plan is particularly conceived for the offensive movement the coach believes in or, better, knows the most about. If the coaches know only motion offense with little or no breakdown, it stands to reason fewer coaches understand teaching individual skills and refinement of those skills because they have been taught by these coaches who have been exposed only to the same five-man game. As a result we have fewer and fewer teachers of the game. This is not meant as a knock at present coaches, but merely fact.

If I was asked what one phase of the individual's game has eroded more and needs attention the most, I would reply footwork. To properly refine one's footwork, balance is strongly stressed or should be. To emphasize my point I will repeat a story that occurred this past year. The occasion was Golden State Warrior practice. I had a group of eight players around me and I was about to describe a drill I was about to introduce. I asked for a basketball and a player handed me a ball. I held the ball up and asked the senior member of the group how many minutes of a 48-minute NBA game did this player suppose he would actually have the ball in his hands. He thought for awhile and said he guessed about 16 to 18 minutes, if he played the whole game. When I said at the most 10% or about 4½ minutes of the 48-minute game, he thought it was incredulous. After I explained that his team could only expect it 24 or less minutes he then understood. I then asked him how many minutes would he play of the 48-minute game with his feet. Not wanting to be so far off again, he thought for awhile and then said 48 minutes. I then asked the group to think about the amount of time they spend refining their footwork as opposed to working on their shot. None admitted to even thinking about the need of improving foot movement. What happened here would happen similarly in the great, great percentage of high school, college, junior college and NBA programs. Little attention is given to this important part of the individual's offensive and defensive play.

Let me dwell on footwork and balance. Is there another word in basketball that has the many connotations of the word "balance"? We talk about floor balance, team shooting balance, body balance, rebound balance, balance in defensive retreat, individual shooting balance, balance between offense and defense and balance of personnel. No one balance I have described above is more important than the balance attributed to and necessary for proper footwork.

How do players improve their footwork and balance? Is it done with a piece of chalk, a vocal exhortation by the coach, through a shaming process from the same coach, threats, pleading, films of just exactly how can it be accomplished? I have never been privileged as a coach to be able to improve skills by any of the above methods. I have tried but failed. Early in my coaching I came to the conclusion that a physical response can only be conditioned by a repetitive act. Once I realized this I devised drills to bring about proper stance, weight carriage and footwork. I employed a fundamental as old as the game, "proper habit is the result of proper repetitive act." In practice I constantly stressed this movement in the various part method teaching drills and supplemented it with a "hands up" type drill that demanded a flexed knee stance and a constant directional change. I will later detail the drill and its "why." In summary, I believe in doing it, not talking about it.

Why is footwork and balance so important and how does it improve the individual's game" A few examples:

A) Shooting. When shooting is discussed at clinics, hand action is strongly stressed, squaring to the basket is a popular advancement. Follow-through is described as absolutely essential and proper hand action, yet without a good base and proper balance, these important fundamentals these clinicians describe would be of much less importance. Good balance must be employed by the shooter. To oversimplify shooting, the shooter is normally faced with two problems on most shots – declinations and deviation. (Two gunnery terms from the Navy.) Declination or depth is of immediate concern to most shooters – deviation or lateral adjustment or float is given little thought. If both declination and deviation are adjustment problems, the shooter's accuracy is bound to lessen. If the shooter could almost totally eliminate deviation, he would then increase his accuracy abundantly. Good balance will accomplish this to a great degree as lateral sway or float by shooters is the result of poor balance in most instances. Obviously if we are only concerned with depth, we have increased our shooting percentage potential. To repeat a good, balanced base is necessary for effective shooting.

B) Creating a Lead. Creating a proper lead in an offensive area is extremely important to an offensive man whether it is the motion offense or a post-type offense. To create this proper lead we must deploy the defensive man into a screen or position him so that he trails the receiver. It is important for most offensive men to receive the ball in specified areas of normal operational zones. The defense is instructed to prevent this reception so footwork and balance is absolutely necessary if the offensive man is to be the shooting, passing or driving threat he is meant to be. If this same offensive man cannot deploy his defensive man properly, he will be operating from unnatural zones which reduces his shooting accuracy, passing efficiency and driving ability.

C) Body Control. Body control is particularly necessary in a fast movement game. "Out of control" is a widely used term to describe a player prone to mistakes in movement; i.e., offensive charge, progress calls, fumbled balls and an inability to properly execute a stop. Without proper weight carriage and footwork balance, good body control cannot be achieved. The body control can only be achieved by a constant practice application and attention. I don't mean to minimize the need of body control in a slower movement game, as it is a must of either tempo, but it is a more apparent need in a faster game.

Without proper balance the ability to quickly stop when running at a fast rate of speed is difficult. Not being able to execute this necessary stop can cause you to lose a chance to receive a pass in a close scoring area. Acceleration will often beat a defensive man, but it is difficult to accelerate if not under control. Changes of direction often fool a defensive man, but balance and footwork can only effectively accomplish this offensive maneuver. Pivots and turns are the result of a good base and low balance and are ineffective if executed in a high position. Rocker steps, step off fakes and other individual skill movements are effective only with the proper balance necessary to refine these movements.

In teaching footwork a coach should realize that ambidextery applies to feet as well as hands. Players are either right-footed or left-footed. They usually prefer a jump shot in one direction (example left against right) over the other. Their drives to the hoop often indicate this subconscious preference. What often happens is that a player will reduce his effectiveness because these preferences are detected in scouting reports. If a player only dribbles right, the defensive problem is greatly reduced because the overplay will cause him great problems. If a player is accurate going only one way and because of a float or sway loses accuracy in the other direction, he will have the same problems with the defense. As ambidextery of hands is stressed by constant encouragement to use the weak hand, drills emphasizing proper footwork should be used on each side of the court to encourage use of either foot in movement, step and shot.

Forward One-on-One Drill

Before going into detail, I would like to explain what we are trying to accomplish: a) how to properly create a lead; b) importance of receiving ball in a normal operational zone; c) various individual moves against pressure defense and insistence of proper footwork; d) distinguishing the type of defense, i.e., soft, aggressive; e) various individual skill moves; and f) reading the type and position of defense and reacting accordingly.

Players are urged to recognize what the defensive man is giving and taking away. He is strongly taught to react to this defensive position rather than presupposing what it will be. Too often a player makes his mind up before he receives the ball and this is often a mistake. Reading and reaction are stressed. The "why" is emphasized so that each player knows what is open and why.

Initially in teaching this drill I will use signals for the defense to denote to them what type (pressure or soft) and what position (overplay right or left) I want employed. I will initially concern myself more with a proper offensive response than with the actual execution of the movement. Again, I am more concerned with reaction and reading in the early stages.

Diagram 1-A

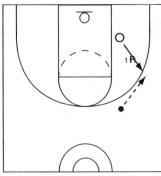

Diagram 1-B

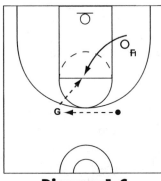

Diagram 1-C

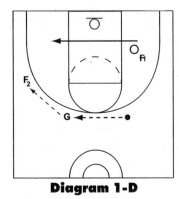

Diagram 1-D

<u>Forwards Basic Position</u>. In Diagram A, F_1 – offensive forward; X – defensive man; and – guard with ball (passer). a) Initial position of forward in creation of lead from guard; b) F_1 gets inside leg across defensive man and moves to receive ball in operation zone (see Diagram B); c) F_1 can come to foul line for blind pig action on guard to guard pass (see Diagram C); d) F_1 can undercut defensive man should ball be reversed to weak side forward (see Diagram D); e) F_1 can empty area should guard beat his man coming down court (see Diagram E).

Note: It is **extremely important** that forward does not move to create the lead as in (b) until he sees his guard's **second** hand go to the ball. This signifies he is picking up the dribble. Timing between passer and receiver can be greatly improved if the receiver is moving toward the ball when guard is **ready** to pass or has **picked up dribble.** This timing will allow for move (e) should guard keep dribble and beat man.

<u>Means for Forward Creation of Lead in His Normal Operational Zone</u>: a) The forward should attempt to get the inside leg across defensive man, hold him for a short count with leg and dart toward operational zone; b) Should defensive man play him high and without ball vision, forward can circle man from inside and receive lead in operational zone (see Diagram F); and, c) Should defensive man overcommit in contesting lead, forward can develop backdoor threat.

It is important forwards learn to develop leads against active, aggressive defensive play. Overplays can disrupt offensive play if forwards are operating in extended areas as passing angles become too sharp, passing lanes too long, and defense can loosen up and invite a longer range shot. The loosened defense reduces passing threat inside and the threat of a dribble minimized.

Normal operational zones for forwards and guards ensure good passing angles, normal distance lanes, and threat of an outside shot or fake shot and drive. Also cutters have better angles and timing on cuts. The importance of normal operational zones should never be minimized in offensive planning nor in defensive strategy and planning.

The **NABC** Drill Book

Practice habits are game habits so create a game condition in this drill and make offense work against game type pressure to create the lead.

Individual Moves Against Pressure Type Defense: The inside foot should always be the pivot foot established by forward after receiving ball. Reasons are: 1) a reverse turn to basket is a real offensive threat **only** if inside foot is the pivot foot; 2) a reverse turn with hand off to circling guard creates a difficult defensive problem; 3) forward is several feet closer to basket when he makes fake to hoop after receiving ball as shown above; and 4) ball is better protected by body against aggressive defense.

If the outside foot is established as pivot foot, an effective reverse turn to basket is reduced, forward can't create good guard motion, several feet are lost in turn toward basket and a front turn can cause defense to steal or tie up the ball.

As stated earlier, the necessity for ambidextery of feet as well as hands so these drills must be developed on both sides of court. Footwork is reversed as inside foot on right side (above) is right foot, on the left side it would be left foot. This drill will ensure development of weaker foot.

Individual Moves Against Softer Defense: a) when defense allows lead without a contest a quarter front turn should be employed (see Diagram G); b) when defense is aggressive – reverse move using a rear turn can loosen defense (see Diagram H). Second foot is reversed toward basket and threat of a reverse drive to basket will loosen defense. Drills against both defenses are used so forward can learn to react against type defense he is confronted with. This is part of the offensive reading that is being taught.

A quarter turn against the soft defense caused defensive man to react to the quick threat of a shot. He is then vulnerable against drive to basket as he moves toward ball.

A reverse turn will cause the aggressive tight defensive man to react to the reverse threat of a drive. Forward comes to immediate shooting position from this fake reverse drive. Defensive man is vulnerable as he recovers from reverse fake and moves toward ball.

Diagram 1-E

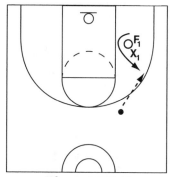

Diagram 1-F

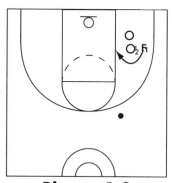

Diagram 1-G

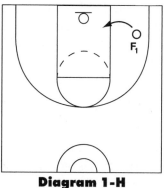

Diagram 1-H

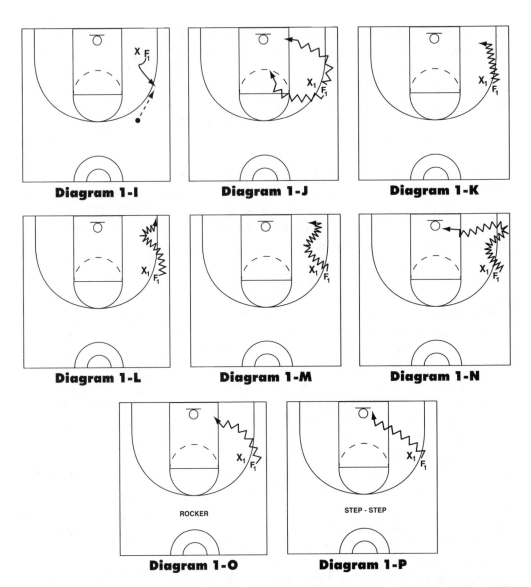

Diagram 1-I   **Diagram 1-J**   **Diagram 1-K**

Diagram 1-L   **Diagram 1-M**   **Diagram 1-N**

ROCKER

STEP - STEP

Diagram 1-O   **Diagram 1-P**

Individual Skill Moves for One-on-One: a) Forward should immediately look toward basket when he receives ball under normal conditions of reception (see Diagram I); b) development of baseline drive and drive over top (to the middle) to the basket (see Diagram J); c) drive to baseline for jump shot – drive to middle for jump shot (see Diagram K); d) drive to baseline for jump shot with pump fake – drive to middle for pump fake jump shot. On this drive the right foot is toward the baseline (see Diagram L); (NOTE: the difference between (d) and (e) is footwork.) e) drive to baseline for step back jump shot and drive to middle for step back jump shot. On this drive the right foot is stepped back toward **sideline**, not baseline as in (d) (see Diagram M); (NOTE: step back is with right foot.) f) a delay off dribble as step back is faked, dribble continues toward baseline and basket (see Diagram N); g) drive to basket after rocker step toward basket. The rocker step is an upper torso and head fake with the lower torso kept in a flexed-knee position. Drive is to baseline to basket and to middle toward basket (see Diagram O); h) drive to basket after step to basket and quick explosion on drive to basket. Baseline or over the middle drive. This move is a quick move as opposed to (g) which is slower, more deliberate move (see Diagram P). (NOTE: It is step with left foot and kick off with right foot as soon as left foot touches floor.)

Reading the Defense and Employment of Proper Move to Combat Defense.

1) Overplays to middle by defense: a) baseline drive to basket, rocker step and step off fakes; b) baseline jump shot and pump fake; c) baseline drive and step back move; and d) baseline drive and dribble delay off step back move.

2) Overplays to baseline: a) drive to middle to basket; b) drive to middle for jump shot and pump fake; c) drive to middle for step back move.

3) Loose Play: a) quick turn to hoop for shot; b) shorten up side lead to force defense play or allow shorter range shot; c) quick turn to hoop for shot; b) shorten up side lead to force defense play or allow shorter range shot; c) quick turn opens up drive potential if defense reacts to turn and potential shot.

4) Aggressive, tight play: a) a reverse turn and drive to the basket; b) a reverse turn and quick look or shot off reverse fake; c) a reverse turn and quick look and fake shot, and drive either way for drive or jump shot; d) use of rocker step and step off moves from (c).

It is imperative that offensive reactions are the result of defensive positions rather than preconceived moves. Too often charging fouls are the result of predetermined movement. Other offensive mistakes are the result of this same predetermined movement so proper reaction to the defense is strongly stressed and demanded in this drill.

Summary:

The basic laws of teaching are readiness, exercise and repetition. Incorporated into those traits is the mental awareness as well as the physical reaction. Mental awareness implies an intellectual appeal. Too often the physical demand by the teacher or coach completely submerges the intellectual appeal. Too often the "how" of doing something is so strongly advanced and the "why" is forgotten. Of the two, it is my belief that the "why" is much more important. It is only simple logic to deduce that a player who understands "why" and "how" to do something will perform more capably than the player who only understands "how." Often a player will get the job done because he understands the "why" and his "how" may not fundamentally be correct. In summary, a teacher should never neglect the intellectual capacity of a player regardless of what he may think of this capacity. An animal can be taught to react, but only a human to think and react.

As I have earlier explained, footwork and the various arts of footwork are mainly neglected at all levels of teaching and coaching basketball. Basketball is a movement game and what is more important than the feet is movement. Exercise and repetition will instill the proper habits of movement. In the drills that have been described in preceding pages, the demand for movement, step offs, stops and turns of either foot diminishes the tendency for the player to overuse or rely upon only one foot. He will learn to execute these footwork moves equally well with either foot. The confidence of a player is often reflected by his effectiveness as a player and the player that can execute his footwork in a superior manner is the confident performer. The great players of the game, Hank Luisetti, Nat Holman, Oscar Robertson, Jerry West, Elgin Baylor were tremendously adept with their foot movements.

Balance, as footwork, must be taught by exercise and repetition. It is more difficult for the taller player to create good habits of balance because his center of balance changes as he grows. The center of balance is a hypothetical line extending laterally through his hips. Too often the growing, clumsy youngster is neglected because he can't immediately perform to the coach's standard. A coach or teacher should recognize one of his most important responsibilities and that is the recognition of the total needs of the player. This taller player's needs for better balance can be remedied by an observant and patient coach.

I am strongly convinced that physical needs are met with physical exercise and repetition. A coach can berate a player with constant admonitions to "stay low", flex those knees and similar reminders, but they are at best a finger in the dike. Only through programmed drills can a dependable game habit reflex be conditioned to properly perform.

Few knowledgeable coaches, if any, would dispute that all motion emanates from a flex-knee position. I have never seen on a basketball court an effective player running stiff-legged, but I have seen many standing in a stiff-knee position. If, then, a player must be in flexed-knee position for quick offensive or defensive movement what do we, as coaches, do about creating this accepted fundamental position of flexed knees? Do we have each player write it 50 times a day on the board, do we expect our voice to instill the reflex, or do we expect a natural physical maturation will take care of this deficiency of the upright player? The coach must recognize the need for constant repetition for instilling the physical habit and increased exercise to condition and strengthen the muscle to allow the player to maintain this position.

An adage in boxing is when your knees stiffen, your head gets hit. Boxing fundamentals and conditioning are very similar to those of basketball. A boxer shadow boxes for interminable periods to build leg strength so that the body can be supported in a flexed-knee position. He keeps his hands up to build muscle support so that he doesn't drop his hands. Correct position of a basketball demands arms and hands up and away from the body. Offensively the hands up ensure better ball reception, fending off an aggressive defensive man with the forearm, readiness for rebounds as well as defensively fending off a screen, slowing a cutter, directing a dribbler and creating a wide extended positioning for a defensive rebound. These defensive maneuvers can only be accomplished with the forearms and the arms up and away from the body. To ensure strength of arm support we use drills. I will describe a drill that will serve the needs of the basketball player with reference to the flexed knees and the raised arms that is as effective as shadow boxing is to the fighter and his needs.

Hands Up Drill. The main purpose of this drill is to create the proper habit of movement on a basketball court. The drill demands a flex-knee defensive type crouch. Weight equally distributed, right foot forward and right hand and arm extended and up. The hand and foot should vary as the drill progresses – equal time for left foot extended and left hand up. The movement is a shuffle with the feet never crossing. The direction of movement is determined by the coach as he gives these directional changes – right, forward, left and rear. The coach should change the tempo of movement constantly and vary the direction of movement often. The alignment of players should be six to eight feet apart spread over an area of the midcourt. The drill commences from this position.

This drill will form proper habit of court movement, build calf and upper leg strength and serve as a stamina and endurance builder. It will help build better body balance as the constant directional changes cause weight shifts. It conditions the feet and toughens them to the rigors of a season ahead. It builds muscle support in the shoulder area which will allow a player to keep his hands up without impairing his shooting accuracy. Arms must be up in shooter's face if good defensive habits are to be taught, but if the arm is tired the hand is often dropped. Shooting accuracy is likewise affected because of this tired arm. Muscle strength and muscle reflex is built through this drill.

This drill should be a part of a team's early conditioning regimen. It is best served in the first part of a practice session. At the college level it should be programmed for the first three weeks of a six-week pre-season program. As in all conditioning drills, the build-up is gradual; i.e., first practice, 4 minutes; two with right foot forward, two with left. Add a minute to a minute and half each day. The team goal is 20 minutes. There is never a stop once the drill commences until the prescribed minutes each day are reached. When a change at the midpoint of time for a particular period is made, there is no stop but merely going from left foot forward to right foot forward or vice-versa. A limit of twelve to 12 to 14 minutes is the highest amount of time I would suggest for the high school player.

Because this drill is extremely demanding physically, I have preferred vocal direction. Some coaches use hand directions – others a player as the directional guide in front of the group. I have found by voice inflection I can exhort them to better movement, forcing a tired, weak arm upward and keeping legs flexed that want to go upright and stiffen. A player learns to gut it out or suck it up, as they say, and that alone is a good practice habit to acquire as the team that practices not to give in to tiredness will win the close tough games. Most players and teams are reduced in efficiency as tiredness sets in and will give in to tiredness if a mental toughness isn't practiced.

I have found this drill rewarding in many ways. A dividend a coach receives by use of this drill is poor practice shooting performance by his team. The arm muscles get extremely tired in the initial stages of the drill as muscle support is being built. This tired arm produces inaccurate shooting. Too often the individual player believes he is ready for the season's opener if he is hitting his shots in the early practices. Sometimes he gets lax about the other phases because of this. If the player is not shooting well, he will generally work harder in other aspects of his game – rebounding, cutting, transition, defense, etc. I would **never** employ this drill during the regular playing season or just prior to it. It is a fine early pre-season drill for specific functions it accomplishes, but it would be counter-productive during the playing season.

Good morale is a team objective or should be. Good morale is associated with mutual respect of the individuals. Pride also is identified with morale. It would be hard to imagine morale without pride. Our Marine Corps was our best example of squad pride, morale and mutual respect. This was based upon the rigors of its training program and its physical demands. Each man knew the other marine endured the demanding drills so he had respect for the pride in his fellow marine. I believe arduous drills intelligently taught can bring about this same team feeling.

Conclusion: What I have attempted to describe are methods to properly teach footwork and balance. I have also emphasized my belief in their importance. Additionally, I have dwelt upon the intellectual appeal to the player as he better understands why he is asked to perform various drills and movements. Conditioning the mind is as important as conditioning the body, so reading and interpreting defenses is stressed. Proper counters to each defense have been explained.

As the high school, junior college and college programs continue the trend toward five-man movement offense and team change-up defenses, less and less time is spent on individual breakdown and needs. Chief among these needs is a refinement of individuals skills, balance and movement.

Defensively, the demand for good balance, quick movement and proper position is absolutely essential for team success. Position is the first fundamental of defense. Position implies feet, or it should. Proper weight distribution and good balance are synonymous with proper feet. Quickness of reaction and movement are totally dependent upon proper body and leg position with a balance of weight equal on each foot. Solid, fundamental defense can only be achieved through these proper footwork fundamentals.

Remember that ninety percent of the game is played without the ball, but only ten percent with it. Teach that 90% as well as the 10%.

Coaching Cues:

All basketball skills are based on footwork and balance, which are only developed through drill repetition. Emphasize mental readiness and physical reaction. Explain how to do the skill and why the skill is important.

Coach:

Coach Pete Newell has developed a reputation as a master teacher of the fundamental skills of basketball – a true basketball educator. He began coaching at the University of San Francisco (1946-50), moved to Michigan State from 1950-54, and finished at the University of California, Berkeley from 1954-60. His teams won the 1949 NIT, the 1959 NCAA, and the 1960 Olympic Gold Medal, and he was national Coach of the Year in 1960. America's "Basketball Guru" was elected to the Basketball Hall of Fame in 1978.

DRILL 2

Ballhandling Warm Up

Purpose:

Teach players to improve ballhandling, especially non-dominant hand dribbling and dual task concentration.

Description:

This ballhandling drill can be used each time a player begins practice, in-season or out-of-season. It can be done alone, but also can be modified to be used with partners. Each segment of the drill is done for 20 seconds with a minimum of three segments (60 sec. = 1 minute). Possible options are:

Solo _Partners_

	Solo	**Partners**
20 sec.	1. Weak hand dribble (keep ball below the knees) and strong-hand juggle (1 tennis ball).	1. Same.
20 sec.	2. Weak hand dribble and 2 ball juggle.	2. Weak hand dribble and stronghand tosses to partner (2 balls – 1 over, 1 under).
20 sec.	3. Weak hand dribble (1 ball) and strong hand dribble (1 ball).	3. Weak hand dribble and stronghand overhand catch with partner.

Coaches can use any creative test of skill and concentration with both hands simultaneously.

Coaching Cues:

Pound the dribble hard, use your whole hand as a suction cup on the ball. Dribbling is a touch skill – force ballhandler to keep visual concentration on another task.

Coach:

Don Meyer is in his 23rd year at the helm of the Lipscomb University Bisons. Some of his accomplishments: reached 600 wins faster than any college coach; selected to NAIA Hall of Fame; National Coach of the Year in 1989 and 1990; head of the largest basketball camp in the nation; and NAIA National Champs in 1986.

Passing Drills
Fall '90 Basketball Bulletin

Purpose:

Teach players to pass and catch effectively in gamelike drills.

Description:

I often hear that passing is a lost art in the modern game of basketball. Coaches, writers, fans, and most important, basketball junkies, seem to agree that while today's players are more skilled all-around athletes, they are not as adept at making the ball appear magically in the hands of a potential scorer.

Many reasons are offered for this deficiency, but one that I rarely hear mentioned is coaches fail to spend enough time teaching and drilling on passing during practice. There seems to be recognition in the coaching fraternity to the fact that passes bouncing off the heads of intended receivers or ricocheting off the top of the backboard on another misguided alley-oop attempt, is the necessary evil that goes along with the evolution of the incredible one-on-one skills possessed by today's players.

I contend that coaches need to spend time during each practice on passing, and while a particular drill will include other aspects of basketball – defense, ball handling, post moves, etc. – the emphasis must be on making good passes. The team must strive for perfection and the coach should accept nothing less than the pursuit of this goal, otherwise there will be no pride in this skill and mediocrity will become habit.

Partner Passing (Diagram A)

Passing, like any skill in basketball, begins with footwork and balance. A good drill to incorporate into your practice plan is one we call "partner passing."

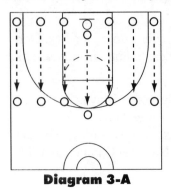

Diagram 3-A

This drill starts with players positioned about 15 feet apart; all should be in good athletic stance, knees bent, feet slightly wider than shoulder width apart, back relatively straight, hands out in front of their body, palms facing the person with the ball. We usually begin by throwing two-handed chest passes.

Points of Emphasis:

♦ Thumbs should snap down, palms end outward.

♦ Full arm extension, lock the elbows on follow-through.

♦ Step into the pass.

- Stay low – weight should end mostly on the front leg – foot should end up in a ballerina position, on toes.
- Good backspin on ball.
- Hard pass.
- Hit the receiver's target.

We have our players throw all types of passes using different pivots and fakes. On bounce passes we stress that the ball should hit the floor at a point three-fourths of the way to the receiver of the pass. The ball should have backspin on it.

Diagram 3-B

Warm Up Passing Drill (Diagram B)

We use this drill as part of our pre-game warm up. Players use chest passes, bounce passes and overhead passes. They start out about 15-20 feet apart and then move in close. Each player has his hands out in front ready to receive a pass and they call out the name of the person they are passing to.

Post Feeds (Diagram C)

The ability of players to make good passes into the post is crucial to any offense. We work on feeding the

Diagram 3-C

post every day. Number 1 passes to 2, who front or reverse pivots (we prefer front pivots as you are moving toward basket), squares shoulders to the rim, puts the ball in triple threat position, and looks to pass to 3, who makes a post move.

Points of Emphasis:

- Start the drill at about 75%, then go live.
- If 1 can't pass to 2, 2 should screen down for 3 and 3 will make the post pass.
- Defensive players should play hard. For the most part, post defender should side front or play behind post.
- Offensive player 2 should receive the pass from 1 above the free throw line. We stress good spacing in our offense.
- We like our players to throw a bounce pass or a soft lob to post players – not a hard straight pass as these are easily deflected.
- Once the passer feeds the post he must move – don't stand and watch.
- Defensive player on wing should double down on the ball.
- The post player should be in a wide stance, legs bent, butt out, pin hand, target hand; or both hands extended in front of his body, and keep his top leg over defense, call for the ball.
- Pass should be away from the defense.

5 on 5 Post Feeds (Diagram D)

Player 1 passes to 2. 2 passes to 4, who passes back to 2. 2 passes to 1. Player 1 takes a few dribbles to create better passing angle and passes to 3. 3 passes to 5,

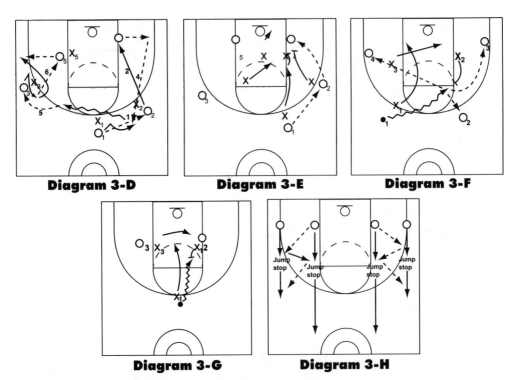

Diagram 3-D   **Diagram 3-E**   **Diagram 3-F**

Diagram 3-G   **Diagram 3-H**

who chins the ball and passes back to 3. Then the drill is live. The defensive players should allow the passes to be made until the drill is live. The wing defenders should double down on the post. The post player should allow the wing defender to double down, then throw the ball back out. The defender on the point person may also double down on the post or may go part way down (see Diagram E). Otherwise the rules are the same as in the post feed drill.

Points of Emphasis:

- ♦ Have the wing offensive players start on the block and create a lead or screen down to free the wing man.
- ♦ Passes should be away from defense.
- ♦ Receivers should let the passer know where they want the ball.
- ♦ Passer must be strong with the ball – triple threat.
- ♦ Passers must set up pass with a ball fake.
- ♦ Perimeter offensive players must move after every pass.
- ♦ All potential receivers of passes must present a good target – make the passer confident that you will get the pass. If the passer is confident that the receiver will make him look good then the passer will be much more effective. Players must **want** the ball.

4-on-3 (Diagram E)

The offensive players must drive to the basket. They can shoot when they get two feet in the paint or you might set up a layup-only rule. At first don't allow the offensive players to cut without the ball. Once they drive-and-dish, they should replace themselves or fill in one of the our original spots. This is an excellent drill for passing off the dribble with either hand, passing out of traffic, making good jump stops, and making correct decisions as to whom to pass to and which type of pass to use. After awhile you can allow the offense to do whatever they want.

Points of Emphasis:

- ♦ Offensive players must be strong with the ball – be aggressive.
- ♦ Passers should jump-stop off the drive, not leave their feet and then decide where to throw the ball. (I realize that many great passes are thrown while in the air – I also know many turnovers occur because the player gets stuck in the air and has nowhere to pass. If emphasis is placed on jump stopping first, the good passers on your team will still make good situations while in the air and your bad passers for the majority of your team – will improve.
- ♦ The offensive players who do not have the ball must be in a good athletic stance ready to receive the ball. Their hands should never be down by their side.

3-on-3 Penetration Drill (Diagram F)

The defensive player guarding 1 allows 1 to drive to the basket. The defenders guarding 2 and 3 must talk and must stop the ball while the other slides to the basket and momentarily plays two people. Player 1 must make a pass to either 2 or 3. The defender who was beat should trap then slide down to a passing lane trying to deflect or intercept's 1 pass.

2-Man Passing (Jump Stops) (Diagram H)

The balls start with the middle people. The wing players start running and when they receive a pass they jump stop. As soon as the middle man releases the ball he begins to run up court and jump stops when he receives return pass from wing player. Once again use a variety of passes.

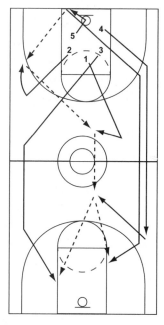

Points of Emphasis:

- ♦ Good jump stops – butt low, feet apart, head back, legs bent, both feet hit at same time.
- ♦ Chin the ball or triple threat position upon receiving pass.
- ♦ Everyone talking.
- ♦ Step into the pass.

Full Court 5-Man Passing (Diagram I)

There are many ways to set up this drill. You can place the players in your press break spots. The key is good v-cuts, coming to meet the ball, and good passes. Player 5 makes a layup – gets the ball out of the net and throws the ball to 2. 2 hits 3 in the middle, 3 pivots and hits 4 who breaks to a point somewhere around the top of the key. 5 and 3 should hesitate at the hash marks until 4 gets the ball and then make their break.

Diagram 3-I

Points of Emphasis:

- Getting the ball in-bounds quickly.
- Sharp v-cuts.
- Good strong pivots.
- Running the lanes hard and wide.
- Run through the pass.
- No dribbling.

You may want to add defensive players – vary the number. This will force the offense to make good decisions and to make good cuts.

Coaching Cues:

The important passing keys to emphasize are:

- Balance and Footwork – players need to get ready to catch the ball before they receive it. Hands should be up, and their legs bent.
- Triple Threat – players should immediately square their shoulders to the rim and get the ball in triple threat position upon receiving a pass on the perimeter. Post players should chin the ball when they receive it or keep it high. They may also turn and face the defense (front pivot or Sikma move). Good pivots create passing angles and protect the ball from defenders. Stay low and cover ground when pivoting.
- Ball Fake – utilize the ball fake as a means of setting up the defense so you can pass around him.
- Step around the defender whenever possible and then throw the pass. Players need to be able to throw a variety of passes – lobs, chest passes, bounce passes, overhead, baseball, off the dribble with either hand and both hands.
- Put backspin on all passes, except the overhead pass which should be a knuckle ball.
- Snap the wrist(s), lock the elbow(s) on follow through. On two-handed chest or bounce passes the thumbs should end up pointing down and the palms of hands pointing outward.
- Step into the pass. Legs should be bent, the back foot should end up on the toes (ballerina position).
- Vision – players need to see the whole court, read the defense quickly and then get rid of the ball. Always pass away from the defense.
- Players must spend more time working on passing and take more pride in this skill.
- Coaches must not condone or allow sloppy passing technique to become habit. Passing should be emphasized in practice and more time needs to be spent polishing this vital aspect of basketball.

I conclude with these thoughts. The next basketball game you watch, at any level, concentrate on how the two teams warm up. Watch closely at how players catch the ball and pass it. Look at their body position, then, following the game, ask yourself how many good or great passers were there in the game. Then ask yourself why.

Coach:

When this article first appeared in its entirety, Steve Spencer was an assistant basketball coach at California Lutheran University.

DRILL 4

Chill Drill

Purpose:

Teach ballhandling, especially dribbling, and improve physical condition.

Description:

Start at the left side of the court (Diagram A) where the baseline and sideline meet. Hold the ball in your right hand. Execute an inside-out move. (Dribble twice on the line in front of you. On the third dribble, take the ball across your body and bounce it to the left of the line in front of your left foot. Explode past an imaginary defender by pushing off your left foot and pushing the ball in front of you back on the line, trying to cover as much ground as possible. Keep your knees bent and your body on the line, moving only the ball. (End at Position A.)

Repeat the inside-out move at point B. (Keep in mind that the ball stays in the right hand.)

Come to a quick (jump) stop where the sideline and halfcourt line intersect (Position C). Execute a reverse or spin dribble, keeping your left foot on the ground. Make sure to reach (hook) with your right leg in order to beat the defender. Pull the ball, with your right hand, being careful not to palm it, as you get the imaginary defender on your back, then switch the ball to your left hand and dribble quickly to Position D.

At point D, pull the ball back beside your left knee, execute two low, quick re-treat dribbles until you reach Position E. The retreat steps help create space against a trap or double-team.

At Position E, execute a quick, low crossover dribble, switching the ball to your right hand.

Take two dribbles and come to a quick (jump) stop at Position F. Execute a half-a-spin move, which is the counter move to the reverse or spin dribble. Do this by pivoting 180 degrees on your left foot and pull the ball until it is directly in front of your right foot. Bounce the ball with force in front of your right foot when your back

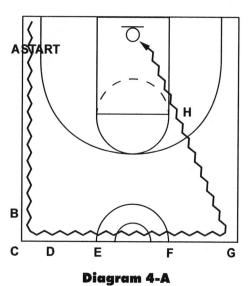

Diagram 4-A

is to the defender. Then explode out by front pivoting on your left foot.

Plant your right foot where the sideline and halfcourt line intersect (Position G) and execute a behind-the-back dribble from your right hand to your left hand, trying to cover as much ground as possible by pushing off your right foot toward Position H.

At Position H, execute a stutter-step to freeze the defender and make a quick, between-the-legs dribble move, switching the ball from your left to your right hand.

You should also practice this drill starting with your left hand so that moves can be perfected with both hands.

Coaching Cues:

Every time you execute a move, accelerate to beat the imaginary defender. Emphasize balance, quickness, and keeping the ball low with vision up the floor. On the pullback dribble, create space from the defender.

Coach:

Ed Schilling, first-year head coach at Wright State University (Ohio), spent seven years as a high school coach before becoming an assistant to John Calipari, at the University of Massachusetts. Their team went to the NCAA I Final Four, and they both went to the NBA - New Jersey Nets.

Individual Skill Development

April-May 1997 NABC Courtside

Purpose:

Teach perimeter players individual offensive skills with the ball.

Description:

As most coaches would agree, individual skill development leads to better players; and, come game time, makes us all look like better coaches. The following drills are some of the perimeter individual workouts we concentrate on at Valparaiso University before and during the season.

Perimeter Workout

- Full-Court – inside out, stutter step, cross-over, behind the back, through the legs, killer cross-over, your option. (The drill starts from half-court as the player goes full speed from half-court and makes his move when reaching the coach at the top of the key.)
- Full-Court Layups – 10 total/3 dribbles (for time, e.g., 1 min. 30 sec.) Player starts from the right elbow and has 3 dribbles to score a layup at the opposite end, rebound his shot, and then do the same thing going back. After 10 layups and two free throws, have player repeat on the left side.
- Penetrate and Pitch – top to wing, wing to top, make five and switch. Player takes two dribbles from top of the key, drawing the defender, while another offensive player on the wing slides to the corner for the three-pointer. The shooter gets his rebound and then goes to the top of the key and repeats. Once five baskets are made, the drill moves to the wing and the player drives to the elbow and passes to the top of the key where the other offensive player takes two steps away from the recovering defender for the three-pointer.
- Seven Spots – one-dribble layups with a catch and pivot. Two free throws and then repeat drill, only this time use

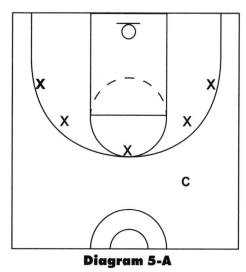

Diagram 5-A

one- dribble jump shots. The X's can be a manager or a chair. The player will curl around the manager or chair and catch the ball, pivot and score. The coach will pass him the ball as he curls around the defender. (This drill is designed to teach players to use only one dribble going from the three-point line to the basket. Remember that the player must pivot, square up, keep shoulders low and explode past defender.)

♦ Dribble Races – place a chair at each freethrow line and one in the half-court circle. Two players will race with one ball around chairs to the opposite baseline. First player to win five is the champion. The races can include the cross-over, inside out, and behind the back.

Shooting

♦ Elbow Jumpers – player must make 15 in one minute (player alternates from right to left elbow).

♦ Seven-Spot Shooting – player must make two shots at each spot in one minute. The seven spots are the same used in the dribbling drill. The shots can be either three-pointers or inside jump shots. The player stays at each spot until he makes both.

♦ Three-Point Shooting – player has 10 minutes to make 100 three-pointers using only one ball and a rebounder. After each made or missed shot, the player must move at least five feet in any direction. Adjust time to your shooter's ability.

♦ NBA Three-Pointers – player has two minutes to shoot as many NBA three-pointers as possible. This drill works on extending the shooter's range.

♦ Pump-Fake 15-foot Jumpers – coach passes to player, who pump fakes, takes one dribble past manager or chair, and then shoots 15-foot jumper. Coach rebounds and the drill is repeated. Player must make ten in one minute.

Coaching Cues:

Focus on doing skills properly and quickly at game speed.

Coach:

Scott Drew and Dave Feuer are both assistants at Valparaiso University (Ind.), where the Crusaders received their first ever NCAA I tournament bid in 1997.

Perimeter Player Offensive Footwork

Fall '87 Basketball Bulletin

DRILL 6

Purpose:

Teach offensive perimeter players to develop correct footwork to get open, catch the ball and face the basket, then pass/shoot/dribble drive.

Description:

Stepping Drill

A. Drill Organization – a line of players at a normal guard position with the ball in the first person's hands and a line off the court with the person first in line set up in the middle of the square formed by the sideline, baseline, free throw lane, and the free throw line extended (see Diagram A).

B. Procedure – 1) the player with the ball initiates the action by dribbling with his outside hand and jump stopping just inside the 3-point line. When the man with the ball stops, the man on the wing takes 3 hard strides toward the basket, changes direction pushing off his left foot, and breaks out to catch the ball. 2) Upon catching the ball the player will make a low front pivot on the left foot into the middle of the court. The objective of the pivot is to activate a defender laterally to make it difficult to defend the drive to the middle, the shot, and the baseline drive (see Diagram B), and to have the balance and strength to execute these maneuvers. Emphasis is placed upon keeping the rear end down, knees bent, and the body weight forward to expedite a drive. 3) In this initial drill the second action is to step across to the baseline and fake a bounce pass to a post player (see Diagram C). 4) The last foot movement is to step to a

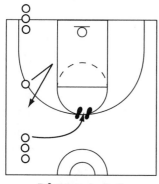

Diagram 6-A

Diagram 6-B

Diagram 6-C

Diagram 6-D

Diagram 6-E

PIVOT FOOT

Diagram 6-F

Diagram 6-G

shooting stance (Diagram D). 5) The player with the ball will then pass to the next man in the guard line and go behind that line. The original guard who passed him the ball will go to the receiver's line (Diagram E). 6) A coach or manager can play the part of a defensive player, as shown in Diagram B to give the offensive player a more realistic look.

C. Improvement should take place in the following offensive footwork fundamentals: 1) The jump stop with the ball by the player dribbling to make the pass. 2) The timing between the guard and the wing as when to move to get open. The wing should be open when the dribbler completes his jump stop. 3) The catch should be made on balance with two hands in a stance that is conducive to a strong front pivot on the left foot into the lane (the only exception to the front pivot, as shown in Diagram F, occurs when the defender attempts to steal the pass and is caught out of position above the ball. The man with the ball would then naturally rear pivot by the defender on his left foot to drive to the goal. 4) The step into the lane with the right foot must provide enough balance to allow the player to pick up the right foot again to start a drive to the right, to step across the defender, or simply to step back and shoot. 5) The balance after the step across (to the baseline) should end in a good stance that allows for driving, stepping back to shoot, or going back to the right.

D. Conclusion: This is our beginning drill for teaching catching on the wing "ready to play." We then move to the other side of the court and work with the right foot as our pivot foot.

Driving Middle off the Step to the Middle

A. Drill Organization is exactly as shown in Diagram A.

B. Procedure: The player catching the ball is now required to catch, front pivot stepping toward the lane, continue to drive middle as though the defense did not respect the step to the middle, and shoot a short jump shot off two feet (Diagrams G and H).

C. Focus is on two areas: 1) Starting the drive without traveling must be watched carefully. We make player

The **NABC** Drill Book

Diagram 6-H   **Diagram 6-I**   **Diagram 6-J**

who travels go again immediately. 2) We work hard on stopping quickly on balance (either front pivot or jump shot) to shoot the ball at the end of the drive.

D. This same maneuver is then done on the right side pivoting on and driving off the right foot.

Driving Baseline off the Step to the Middle

A. <u>Drill Organization</u> is as shown in Diagram G.

B. <u>Procedure</u>: The player is to front pivot into the middle of the floor and then step across with the right foot and drive baseline, stop on two feet, and shoot (Diagram I). This situation would present itself in a game when the defensive over-reacts to the step to the middle (Diagram I).

C. Our <u>Focus</u> again is on a strong first step without traveling and on balance on the shot off two feet. We teach two different shots at the end of the drive: 1) The first shot is the standard short jump shot when you get the defense totally off balance on the first step. 2) The second occurs when you get half a step on the defense to get penetration to the gaol, but the defender has enough balance and position to make a play. The offense must now end his drive in a jump stop protecting the ball with his body to attempt the shot. We teach our players to turn as they stop to seal the defender on their back for the power shot (Diagram J).

D. <u>Repetition</u> must take place on both sides of the floor.

The Next Drill In The Sequence Is Live One-on-one From The Wing From Both Sides Of The Court

A. <u>Drill Organization</u> is exactly as in the previous drill except a defender is added guarding the wing player. The defense is full go trying to keep the ball out of the wing man's hands.

B. The offense must get open to receive the ball as close to the 3-point line as possible and use the footwork practiced in the preceding drill to get his shot.

C. If the player with the ball makes a move but does not get a good shot, he passes the ball back to the guard and gets open again to receive the ball.

D. Emphasis is placed on proper footwork and balance. Any mistake by the offensive player is corrected when it occurs. Bad shots are not permitted. Rebounding is a part of the game. If no fundamental mistakes occur, the action stops when the defense stops the offense and gets the rebound under control. No live drill should let the defense off easy.

In conclusion, we have found these drills most helpful in improving our players' balance and quickness against pressure defenses. We use the stepping drill without the live defense every day of our pre-season practice. We will practice getting open and playing one-on-one from the wing with live defense every day (except the day prior to games) almost the entire season.

We have found that we are never as good as we can be getting open, squaring up, starting drives both right and left, using either foot as a pivot foot, and ending drives on balance to shoot or pass. We have seen our players' confidence soar as they learn to use their feet correctly on offense.

Coaching Cues:

Be effective in developing balance and quickness against pressure. Focus on V-cuts to get open, square to the basket, and be able to pass/shoot/dribble drive.

Coach:

Eldon Miller formerly coached at Ohio State and has developed a successful program at the University of Northern Iowa.

DRILL 7

Big Man Drills/Moves
Winter '79 Basketball Bulletin

Purpose:

Teach post players the necessary offensive skills and moves to be effective as an inside player.

Description:

In the past seven years, our system has been extremely effective with the use of two big men in the same lineup together and then were fortunate enough to win the NCAA National Championship with two big men.

Despite the ever-present criticism that this type system would not work, we worked extremely hard with our big men on a daily basis through various fundamental drills and inside moves.

Toward the end of each season you can actually see the big man drills being put effectively to work in game situations. The secret is: 1) repetition through hard work in the drill sessions each and every day; 2) patience with slow developers; and 3 (a dedicated commitment to the two-big-man system. The following are drills and moves that the big men in our program work on every day:

♦ Mikan Drill. Continuous hooks with each hand. Right hand hook, left hand hook, continuous.

♦ Tip Drill. Throw ball on board, tip with right hand and finish with a basket. Then use left hand tip. Work up to 5 or 6 tips with each hand.

♦ Rebound-Stuff Drill. Throw ball on board, go up with one hand and stuff. Use both hands. Then go up and stuff with both hands. (3 sets)

♦ Beat-the-Rim. Throw ball on board, go up and get it, then beat the ball against the rim before coming down. Beat the rim twice, then thrice.

♦ Power up. Throw ball on board, go up and get it, then bring it down, keep the ball at shoulder level. DO NOT BRING IT TO YOUR WAIST. Then go up very strong and shoot a power layup off the glass.

♦ Pump Fake – Power Layup. Same as power layup, only this time use a pump fake with the head and ball. Do both these drills on each side of the basket.

♦ Superman Rebound Drill. Player starts outside free throw lane. Put the ball on the board above the basket at an angle and go rebound it on the other side of the lane with both feet outside the lane. Pull ball into chin. Then throw it back to the other side and go get it. Do this continuously for 30 seconds. Work up to a minute.

- **Two-Ball Superman Drill**. Place a ball on each block. Begin by picking up a ball and power move it to the hole; quickly go get the other ball and power it to the basket; continue this sequence for 30 seconds. Work up to a minute. You will need two other people to help you with this drill.

Big Man Moves

- **Low Side/Power Move**. Post up big and wide on the block. The defense is 3/4 fronting you on the high side. Ward him off with your highside arm, receive the pass, and power move straight to the basket without a dribble. Then, utilize one dribble in your power move. GO UP STRONG! Do this on both sides.
- **High Side Lane Hook**. Defense is now 3/4 fronting on the low side. Ward him off with the low side arm, spread wide, give a BIG target, receive pass, and then one step in the lane for the baby hook. Do this on both sides.
- **Lob Pass Play**. Defense is totally fronting. Get position on the block. When the lob pass is thrown, keep both hands high; then when the ball is directly overhead, release from the defensive man and go get the ball – Power Layup. Keep hands high to avoid a pushing off call by the official.
- **Turn and Face**. Defense is playing completely behind. Establish position with good, big post-up, then if you feel pressure – receive the pass, pivot and face your man. Drive him right or left, or shoot the jumper. If you feel no pressure, receive the pass then, and shoot the quick turn-around bank shot.

Coaching Cues:

Work hard and emphasize quick repetitions daily, be patient with big players, and commit to using big players.

Coach:

Joe B. Hall was a longtime assistant coach at Kentucky under Adolph Rupp. After taking over as head coach, his teams won two national championships using the double post system.

DRILL

8

Triple Jump Stop

Purpose:

Teach players all types of legal stops; stride (one, two count on both feet), jump (one count on both feet), and the triple (one count, one foot). The third stop teaches players to increase the distance traveled without dribbling or with only one dribble (Rule 4 - Traveling section).

Description:

Use only the triple jump stop.

◆ Pass - catch with both feet in the air. Player passes ball to self (back spin pass) or receives ball from partner. Catches ball while in the air, lands on one foot, jumps off that foot and lands on both feet at once (can't lift either foot).

◆ Dribble and catch ball in air off the dribble, land on one foot, jump off that foot and land on both feet at once.

◆ Pass - catch with one foot on the floor, jump off that foot, and land on both feet at once.

Coaching Cues:

Catch the ball with both feet in the air – land on one foot, jump and land with a jump stop. Catch ball with one foot on the floor – jump off foot and land with jump stop.

Coach:

Thirty-four year coaching veteran, Gene Mehaffey is the head coach at Ohio Wesleyan University. The 1998 NCAA III National Championship winning coaching, Mehaffey has accumulated 508 wins during his college tenure.

Bull in Pen

Purpose:

Teach players to pass under pressure and to defend the ball handler.

Description:

Two offensive players are placed 15-18 feet apart with a defender in the middle. Defender flips ball to offensive player and closes out to defend (trace ball, keep a gap, pressure the pass, get a deflection while staying in stance). Offensive player must pass to offensive player—can only use one pass fake and/or one dribble. When pass is made, defender must close out to ball and repeat sequence. Defender stays in the middle for 20 seconds, then rotates out to offense.

Coaching Cues:

Passer - take ball to defender, use only vertical fakes, accurate quick passes.
Receiver - give a target, maintain 15-18 feet apart.
Defender - close out to prevent drive, move feet, stay in stance.

Coach:

Jim Harrick is the head coach at the University of Rhode Island and the former head coach at UCLA (where he won the 1995 National Championship). Previous to coaching at UCLA, he coached at Pepperdine University.

DRILL

10

Post Passing Drill

Purpose:

Teach post players to catch, make post moves, and pass from the post position as they read the opponent's defenders (read and react). Teach defensive players to double team a post player and rotate to the ball on passes from the post.

Description:

The drill is carried out on the halfcourt with five offensive players (2 post players and 3 perimeter players) and five defensive players. The defense allows the first pass inside to the post as shown in Diagram A, where the offensive post player goes one-on-one (no double team).

In Diagram B, the entry pass is made the defensive team double teams the post player with the ball. The post player should locate and find the open teammate. Once the entry pass is allowed inside, both offense and defense is "live." In this sequence, X_3 double teams O_5.

Drill begins with the defensive team huddling and deciding on a defensive strategy (no double team or double team from the defensive 1, 2, 3 or 4 position). The teams rotate from offense to defense to off the court – three teams can be kept very active.

Diagram C shows X_1 doubling down from the top; Diagram D shows X_2 on a weakside double team; and Diagram E depicts a post double team from X_4.

Coaching Cues:

Allow the first entry pass, then go "live" offense and defense. Simulate all offensive and defensive strategies for defensive and offensive post play. On the post pass, have perimeter players read the defense and practice moves without the ball to get open for a return pass.

Coach:

Mike Beitzel, Hanover College Basketball Coach, has led the Panthers to several playoff appearances, including two straight NCAA III tournaments. In seventeen years as a college head coach, his teams have had fourteen winning seasons. Coach Beitzel has also coached at Northern Kentucky, Wooster College, Cincinnati, Ohio State, and the United States Naval Academy. Mike is also active on the NABC Research Committee.

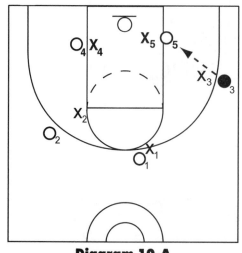

Diagram 10-A

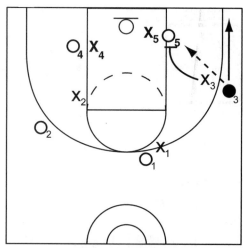

Diagram 10-B

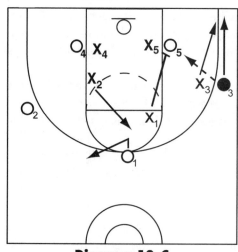

Diagram 10-C

Diagram 10-D

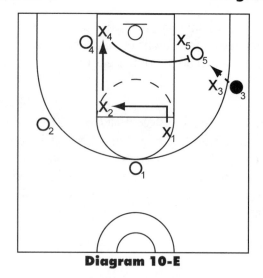

Diagram 10-E

Triangle Passing Drill

Purpose:

Teach players to catch, seal and finish their offensive move/shot to score in traffic.

Description:

The passer is stationed at the FT line. He passes to one of the two receivers who are on the block (Diagram A). The receiver must catch, seal off the defender who is in the lane and finish/score under pressure (Diagram B). Immediately after each score, the ball is passed (outlet) to C_1 or C_2 and action is repeated. Each player takes 3 - 5 repetitions and rotates (Diagram C).

Coaching Cues:

Focus on hi-low passing (get open, catch and face, protect ball, and use bounce pass). Post players on the block need to step into or pivot into the lane, give a target, catch and protect ball with their body, take the ball to the glass and convert the score while absorbing defensive contact. Defender X deflects the pass and defends post after pass.

Coach:

Jeff Jones is one of the new rising stars in college basketball, head coaching in the challenging Atlantic Coast Conference at the University of Virginia, where he also played.

Diagram 11-A

Diagram 11-B

Diagram 11-C

DRILL 12

Dribble Follow

Purpose:

Teach players proper offensive spacing, ball handling, and cutting for motion offense.

Description:

Begin with ball at wing and one other offensive player in the corner, as shown in Diagram A. Also shown is the dribble up, face cut by 1 and the return pass to 2, who relays the ball. 1 dribbles up hard, stops and steps-through on the pivot, passes back to 2 and makes a front (face) cut inside the imaginary defender for a layup.

Use same set and move in Diagram B – dribble up, step-through pivot by 1, ball-fake to 2, with 2 backcut to basket for layup.

The drill progression then proceeds to 2-on-2 where offensive player with ball dribbles up with offensive partner following for spacing. They then read defense and play live.

Coaching Cues:

Drill 2-on-0 until moves are automatic, then add two defenders to work on reaction to defense.

Coach:

Jimmy Tillette became the new head coach at Samford University in 1997 after seven years as an assistant. He has also assisted at Tulane and Mississippi State. Coach Tillette is known for his knowledge of motion offense.

Diagram 12-A   **Diagram 12-B**

Quick Drills
Spring '80 Basketball Bulletin

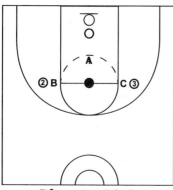

Diagram 13-A

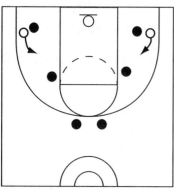

Diagram 13-B

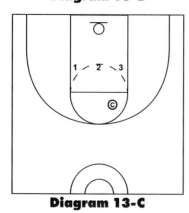

Diagram 13-C

Purpose:

To teach players to convert quickly by learning to think and act quickly in drills.

Description:

Conversion is the most important reaction in the game today. Anything we can do as coaches to make players quicker is very important. We probably spend less time on trying to condition a player's mind to react to different situations quickly. I think we can make players quicker by getting them to think quicker; getting them to think faster; getting them to think – period!

Drills to Improve Player's Reaction

Shooting: Time – competition – combination of both.

Time – make five shots from the free throw line within 20 seconds. Rebound own shots. Two ball shooting drill (see Diagram A). Player at foul line takes a shot, steps, fakes, and a manager hits him with a pass. Managers rebound. 30 seconds (build to 60 seconds).

Competition and Time – Two players (see Diagram B) from a designated spot. The player who makes the most shots is the winner. 20 seconds. Rebound own shots.

Rebounding: Two on one rebound drill (Diagram C). Three players are in rebounding area. Coach puts ball on board. All three players go after rebound. The one who gets the ball must put it in the basket, while the other two try to stop him. We do not allow rebounder to dribble. We emphasize the 3-point play. We tell the players not to worry about the contact. The ball is live until a basket is scored or it goes outside of the lane. The coach should be inside the foul line for best control of the drill. Two minutes.

A, B, and C are already in the blockout position facing the ball in the middle. At the coach's signal, 1, 2 and 3 will try to get the ball. A, B, and C must move with them, keeping contact and not allowing the offense to get the ball for at least five seconds. The drill can also be set up so that A, B, and C are facing their men. Now, at the coach's signal, they will have to use the rear turn to make contact and then hold it for five seconds.

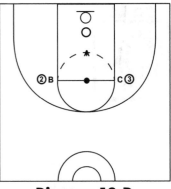

Diagram 13-D

Passing: Pass, Return and Handoff (Diagram E). The basic passing drill that we use to start each of our practices is outlined in Diagram E. We set this drill up on the four corners of the foul lane with at least three players on each corner. We started out with 1 and 3 each having the ball. Player 1 passes to 2 and starts toward him with a return. When 1 catches the return, he goes in front of 2 and flips the ball back to 2. 1 then goes to the end of 2's line. The action between 3 and 4 is simultaneous and the same. This action is subsequently repeated from corner to corner in the same direction and simply consists of three things – pass, return and hand off.

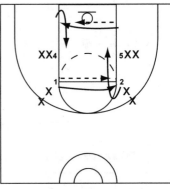

Diagram 13-E

When the players are able to move two balls efficiently, as third ball can be added and eventually a fourth. As soon as they can handle three balls, we have them change direction by one of the coaches calling out change. When this is done, the players having the balls at that time reverse them and execute the same action in the opposite direction. We feel the close confines of the lane are excellent for the development of quick passing and cutting while changing direction does a lot for reaction.

Coaching Cues:

Think quick and be quick. Do skills properly and quickly.

Coach:

Bob Knight of Indiana University has achieved nearly every coaching distinction – 11 conference titles, five Final Fours, one NIT championship, three NCAA championships, and an Olympic Gold Medal. He also coached at West Point as the youngest major college coach in history, where his teams played in four NIT tournaments in five seasons. He was inducted into the Basketball Hall of Fame in 1991.

DRILL 14

Lucky 7 Layups

Purpose:

Teach players to communicate, pass, catch, and shoot layups in competitive situations.

Description:

A group/team of players are on a fullcourt with six baskets, as shown in Diagram A. A player with a ball is at each basket. The designated shooters are in the large center circle in the middle of the court. The object of the drill is to score seven consecutive layups. Each middle player must call a player's name at a basket, sprint toward that basket to receive a pass, return pass to the basket passer who again passes to the shooter for a layup (see diagram) with 0_1 as the passer. After each layup the shooter must call a name/use a passer on the opposite half-court. Shooters must use each passer once during their lucky seven and should receive the first pass outside the 3-point line distance. Shooters and passers switch after all reach 7 or after one reaches 7.

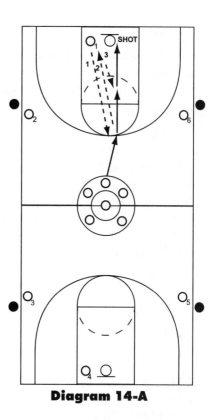

Diagram 14-A

Coaching Cues:

Focus on fundamentals of

- ◆ passing – quick, accurate, pass with a ping (not too hard or too soft); may designate type of pass;
- ◆ catching – use both hands, soft hands, catch with eyes;
- ◆ layup shots – two hand catch, chin ball near outside armpit, take up with two hands, high jump, dunk or use the glass; may designate layup (right, left, cross-under, baseline approach, etc.)

Coach:

Heather Kirk, Assistant Women's Coach at the United States Military Academy at West Point.

DRILL
15

Shoot the Hand

Purpose:

Teach offensive shooting concentration with defensive pressure and defensive closeout plus one-on-one skills for both offense and defense.

Description:

See Diagram A. Place three players in each group: passer, shooter, rebounder. Passer passes to shooter and follows to contest shot and blockout, becomes next shooter, shooter follows to become next rebounder. In Diagram B passer becomes next shooter, rebounder follows pass to contest, rotation continues.

Drill can be expanded to

♦ shooter uses lift fake and penetrates to basket;

♦ shooter uses lift fake and hard dribble to pull-up jumper.

For good competition, go one-on-one live, keep score – losers run. Limit offense to three dribbles. To make them use good foot fakes and dribble drive techniques, defense must block out and play through the rebound.

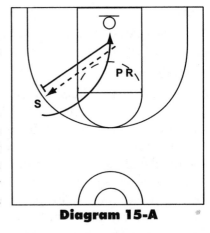

Diagram 15-A

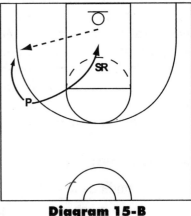

Diagram 15-B

Coaching Cues:

Use correct closeout skills, contest the shot without fouling, and block out on defense. Offensive player, move to receive the pass (v-cut), set up for the shot, and concentrate on the basket (not the defender).

Coach:

Rick Samuels has been coach at Eastern Illinois University for 18 years – the winningest coach in school history, a 1992 NCAA I tourney participant. Basketball program graduation rate among top 10% of NCAA I schools. Rick is a longtime member of the NABC Research Committee.

Two-Ball
Motion Shooting

Purpose:

Teach players to take game shots from motion offense cuts.

Description:

Each player has a ball with a partner and two coaches or managers as feeders at each basket. Diagrams A, B, and C show three motion variations with both shot opportunities used at each screen and cut. The drill starts with both players at the head of the shooting lines with a live ball, triple threat 15 - 18 feet apart. Both players make a crisp "skip" pass to feeders on opposite side of court. The drill can be run on both sides of the court with the motion moves of

- downscreen fill and flare;
- downscreen curl and fill;
- backscreen curl and fill;
- backscreen flare and fill;
- backscreen fill and flare;
- backscreen backcut and fill.

Both players follow their shot, rebound and score, then switch lines.

Coaching Cues:

Screener – set a good legal screen and read your partner's cut. Cutter – wait and use a controlled v-cut to cut close to the screen. Shooters – catch the ball in balance and shoot "game shots at game spots at game speed."

Coach:

Dan Hays, an Albuquerque native, Head Coach and Athletic Director at Oklahoma Christian University (448-266 record as a head coach, 310-157 at OCU in 14 years.) Recognized as an organizational/fundamentals oriented coach. Will be inducted into NAIA Hall of Fame in 1998.

Diagram 16-A

Diagram 16-B

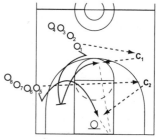

Diagram 16-C

Pacer Shooting

Purpose:

Teach players to pass, catch, and shoot in a competition situation.

Description:

In Diagram A, three players are placed at each basket with two balls. Each player shoots, follows shot for the rebound, and passes to the free player. After passing, he must hustle back and make a v-cut into shooting position facing the basket. A player may choose to shoot a 2-point or 3-point shot. The goal is 50 points in one minute.

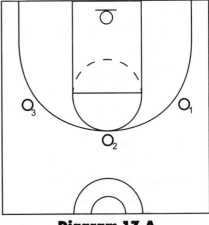

Diagram 17-A

Coaching Cues:

Crisp and accurate passes, catch the ball ready to shoot, communicate with the passer, shoot with balance, hustle any rebounds. Coach can designate penalty if goal is not met, e.g., run a sprint.

Coach:

Dave Odom is a successful head coach at Wake Forest University, where his teams are perennial title contenders. They are noted for their excellent team play and individual skills.

DRILL 18

Multiple Cuts Shooting Drill

Purpose:

Teach players to properly shoot the basketball when coming off screen situations.

Description:

Diagram A will show the drill set up, and an explanation will follow. We start out as a three man drill and eventually get up to four and five men later on. 1 is the passer, 2 is the screener, and 3 is the shooter. We have players fill all the spots, but a coach or a manager could actually fill the 1 spot.

Diagram B will show 1 executing a "pop-out" cut for the jump shot; the explanation will follow: 1 keys the drill by starting the dribble or slapping the basketball. 2 takes one step on and downscreens for 3 who v-cuts one step away from the direction he is going to cut and then pops off the screen to the wing. 1 passes to 3 for the shot coming off the screen. If the shot is missed, 2 will rebound it and put the basketball through the hoop with a power lay-on.

In Diagram B we show a "pop-out" cut which we run when the defender is run into the screen. Now in Diagram C we show a flare cut, which we run when the defense fights the screen into the middle on a one-man-removed fashion.

In Diagram C, the drill is all exactly the same except that 3 is running a flare away from the defender. 3 has to read how he is being defended.

Diagram D will show a curl cut, which we run when the defense fights the screen over the top. Here we see the curl by 3 for the short jumper in the middle. 3 and 1 both must read the situation so that they are on the same page with each other.

In Diagram E we are going to add one more offensive player to be put opposite of 3. Diagram E will

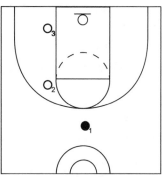

Diagram 18-A

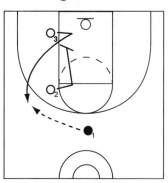

Diagram 18-B

Diagram 18-C

show what we call a multiple cut. On the multiple, 3
sees his defender cheating his cut coming off 2's
downscreen, so 3 runs off a baseline screen out the
other side. The screen is set by 4. Now 3, off the
multiple can flare, pop-out, or curl depending on how
his defender tries to play him. All of our offenses vs
man have these options.

Diagram 18-D

First we teach the drill and cuts with no defense.
The first defender we add is to the receiver of the
screen, then to the screener, and eventually to the
passer as well. Thus creating in the end a 3-on-3 situation. This is also a drill we use to teach our players
how to fight through screens. We do not switch, so
this becomes a great defensive drill for us as well.

Diagram 18-E

Critical Cues:

1. The Downscreen. When we downscreen we want
   the screener to get to the screening position as
   quickly as possible. We do not want him to walk
   down. He must get down there quickly. When
   the screen is set we want to set the screen with a
   two-foot stop with the feet wider than shoulder
   width by a considerable amount. We like the
   screener's knees flexed to about 110° for a lower center of gravity, thus en-
   abling him to set a strong screen. The screener should fold his arms palms
   down on the chest. Elbows stay in and palms flat.

2. V-Cut. One or two steps at the most opposite of the direction that you will be
   cutting. Too big of a v-cut is as bad as none at all. We teach the receiver of the
   screen to be facing the screener as the screener sets the screen. The receiver of
   the screen must be in a "ready" position with a low center of gravity so that he
   can cut hard. On the v-cut the screener plants the inside foot (the foot nearest
   the basket), pushes off to explode off the screen.

3. The Rub. The screener and the receiver of the screen must rub outside shoulder
   to inside shoulder as the receiver comes off the screen. This forces the defender
   to be hit by the screen or at least to have to go around it. If there is a gap
   between the two, the defender can sneak through the screen with the cutter.

4. Crouch Cut — Target. The receiver of the screen must come off the screen in
   what we call the crouch. The crouch involves turning towards the basketball by
   twisting the upper body on that direction with a two-hand target. The cutter
   should be low with the upper body twisted on such a manner that just a quarter
   turn is all that is needed to square up. As the cutter cuts he should be giving the
   passer a two-hand target, and he should be cutting hard to gain separation
   from the defense. Anything done at less than game speed is basically worthless.

5. Receiving the Basketball. We like our players to receive the basketball with a

two-foot stop squared up to the basket in triple threat position. The second the basketball gets on their hands, they should be ready to shoot. As the cutter is in the crouch position he times a slight hop off of his inside foot so that as he catches the basketball his feet are hitting the ground at basically the same time. The hop should also make a quarter turn to the basket, thus squaring the shooter up. This hop off the inside foot is not a high hop; it is shallow and quick.

6. The Pass. Must be on the mark; directly to the target. A bad pass can cost the shooter and the team a basket. We like the one-hand push pass, but more importantly we want the task completed efficiently.

7. Shot Mechanics. All shooters must shoot the basketball properly, executing all fundamentals of proper shooting techniques.

8. The Rebound. The rebound should be made aggressively and the basketball should be captured with two hands. As the shot is in the air good screen-out position should be established – wide base with the feet, tail down, back straight, elbows bent 90° with hands open and fingers to the ceiling.

9. The Power Layin. Shot off both feet with shoulders square to the baseline, and powering up to the basket aggressively.

These fundamentals must be executed at all times throughout the drill.

Coach:

Jeff Reinland is head men's coach at Walla Walla Community College. He had a successful playing career in high school, community college, and at Eastern Washington University. Jeff has been a high school coach as well. His teams are exceptionally disciplined and well-grounded in fundamental skills.

DRILL 19

30 Baskets

Purpose:

Teach players improved shot preparation and more effective shooting, passing, and communication.

Description:

As seen in Diagram A, the drill starts with rebounders R_1 and R_2 under the basket and five shooters located at the five spots around the 3-point line. Three balls are used as shooters call rebounder's name to receive a pass, shoot, and count the total made baskets. When made basket count reaches 5, shoot-

Diagram 19-A

ers rotate clockwise until 30 total baskets are made (six rotations). The 30 Basket Drill can be carried out at both ends of the floor, simultaneously, with seven more players. Each group of seven can compete against other groups. The winner may change baskets as the losing group(s) carry out a penalty (five pushups, five situps, run, etc.) before they change baskets to start another game.

Coaching Cues:

Be prepared to shoot (hands ready, feet ready), call passer's name, v-cut to receive the pass, rebounders make quick and accurate passes (may designate the pass) after chasing down rebounds and made baskets. Be quick, but don't hurry your pass or shot.

Coach:

Dan Hipsher has been head coach at the University of Akron for two years, after coaching at Stetson (FL), Wittenberg (OH), and spending nine seasons under Don Donoher at Dayton (OH) and two years at Miami-Dade (FL). Coach Hipsher has developed a reputation as a "program builder."

Six-Man – Five-Ball Shooting

Purpose:

Teach players to find the open man (passing) and shoot without dribbling, follow your shot to rebound, then find the open man. High volume shooting.

Description:

Players are spread on the halfcourt, as seen in Diagram A. Each player will shoot, follow their shot and rebound the made or missed shot, then pass to the open player, either directly or after a dribble outlet. Players must communicate and operate in traffic.

Coaching Cues:

Work together – talk, cut, shoot, and pass. Shoot as you catch the ball. Make accurate, quick passes. Follow your shot.

Coach:

Bruce Haroldson, a fourteen-year head coach at Pacific Lutheran University, has been a college coach for 30 years (seven, assistant at Arizona State; four, head at Mesa State (CO); and five, head at Montana State). United States Olympic Sports Festival Assistant in 1990.

Diagram 20-A   **Diagram 20-B**   **Diagram 20-C**

DRILL

21

50-Point Shooting

Purpose:

Teach players to shoot all types of game shots in competitive situations.

Description:

Players are grouped as three players per basket, each with a ball. All three players shoot at the same time, using the "spin and catch" technique (toss a two-hand underhand pass to self with backspin so that it bounces from the floor up into the shooting pocket). The goal of each player is to reach 50 points first. The first player to hit 5 shots ends each phase – for example: player A (5), player B (4), player C (2) means their individual scores are 5, 4, and 2 at that point.

The four drill phases are:

♦ shooting with no dribble;

♦ shooting off the dribble;

♦ using backboard shots; and

♦ shooting 3-point shots.

After each phase, all three players then shoot five free throws, one at a time. Repeat process for all four phases. After phase 4, each player will shoot up to 15 FT individually. This ends the drill with pressure free throws when the first player in each group reaches 50 points. Players track their own score.

Coaching Cues:

Make a good "spin and catch" pass to yourself, shoot game shots in your range. Be aware of teammates when shooting to ensure basket is clear (may use shot fakes).

Coach:

Steve Alford had a legendary championship playing career at New Castle (Ind.) High School; Indiana University, with legendary coach Bob Knight; as a member of the 1984 United States Olympic team; and in the NBA. He was renowned as a pure shooter. Since then, he began his coaching career at Manchester College (Ind.), where he spent four years (three NCAA III tourney appearances), and now coaches at Southwest Missouri State University.

Full Court Layup/ Shooting Drill

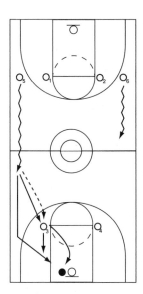

Diagram 22-A

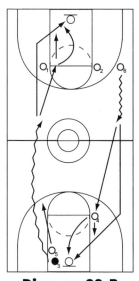

Diagram 22-B

Purpose:

Teach players basic offensive skills of shooting, passing, catching, dribbling and pivoting while also conditioning.

Description:

A full court drill that includes running, ballhandling, shooting and pivoting. This drill requires team concentration and encompasses many full-court offensive skills.

Coaching Cues:

Full court dribbling (head up, find the target), jump stop before using the two-hand chest pass, cut to basket with a push off outside foot (and 45° angle for layup), and use proper layup technique (under control, foot in the lane, high jump).

Coach:

Norm Stewart has been a head college coach for over 36 years and is one of the few coaches in basketball to record over 700 victories, which places him in the elite all-time top 10. He coaches at his alma mater, the University of Missouri, and was 1994 National Coach of the Year. Stewart's teams have won eight league championships and six conference tourney titles.

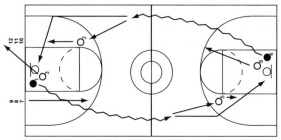

Diagram 22-C

Offensive Fundamental Drills   **47**

Daily Half-Dozen
Spring '86 Basketball Bulletin

Purpose:

Teach players ballhandling, shooting, and conditioning using a full-court, progressive fast break drill series.

Description:

Practice time is something that we never seem to have enough of so I feel that the drills used should always accomplish as many things as possible and create habits that will be beneficial in game situations. The drills that follow emphasize shooting, conditioning and ballhandling on the run at game speed, as well as the fundamentals of the fast break. These drills are progressive and the players should move continuously from one to the next without pause. They should also be run at full game speed.

To begin, divide the squad in half and position the players as shown in Diagram A. The continuity of the drills is best achieved when an even number of players are used, but this is not

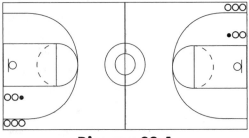

Diagram 23-A

necessary. Two balls are used and the player in the inside line at each end of the floor begins with a ball.

Drill #1 – Chest Pass

This first drill may be used as a warmup for the remaining drills or run at full speed. The drill begins on a signal from the coach and the players move in pairs down the floor making as many two hand chest pass exchanges as possible. When they reach the opposite end the ball is passed to the first player in the inside line to start back down the floor with his partner. The players change lines for the return as shown in Diagram B.

Diagram 23-B

Coaching Points:

1. Keep good spacing.
2. Passes should be accurate and easy to handle.

Drill #2 – Pass Ahead

Lines should be repositioned as shown in Diagram C. This should be done without stopping the drill and is no problem once the players run the drill a couple of times. The player in the outside line should come for the outlet pass, calling out "outlet" to alert his teammate to his position. The inside player should use a blast-out dribble with left/right hand. The outside player seeing the inside man move up floor should turn and sprint down the outside lane. When the dribbler sees his teammate break out ahead he should pass ahead over the defense to the player cutting to the basket (see Diagram C).

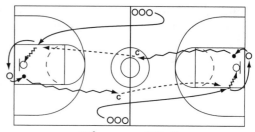

Diagram 23-C

Coaching Points:

1. Rebounder should look for the outlet pass.
2. Use hard blast-out dribble moving straight upcourt.
3. Pass should be made on an arc into the lane area bouncing about the foul line.
4. Passer should avoid the charge after the pass.
5. Layup should be shot under control with the shooter going up strong and staying on the floor after the shot.

Drill #3 – Foul Line Jump Shot

The inside player rebounds either a made or missed shot and outlets the ball to the player coming for the outlet from the outside line. The player receiving the outlet pass should speed dribble with left/right hand to the foul line for a jump shot. The player throwing the outlet pass should follow the pass and sprint down the outside lane and make a good cut to the basket, as shown in Diagram D.

Coaching Points:

1. Rebounder should make proper pivot, keep ball high and make good outlet pass.
2. Outlet should be coming to the ball and calling "outlet."
3. Outlet should make first dribble in anticipation of defense in position to take charge, then speed dribble left/right down the middle of the court.

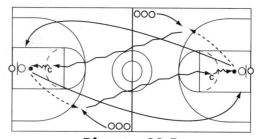

Diagram 23-D

4. Player making outlet pass should follow the pass and sprint down the outside lane on fast break.
5. Cut to the basket by player in the outside lane should be on a line of 45 degrees to the basket creating good position to stop and take wing jump shot or receive pass for the layup.

6. Middle man should stop at the foul line under control using a jump shot.

Drill #4 – Layup

Same as Drill #3 except middle man makes an air pass or a bounce pass to the cutter for a layup after coming to a jump stop under control at the foul line. The passer should slide to the side of the pass setting up for a possible return pass as shown in Diagram E.

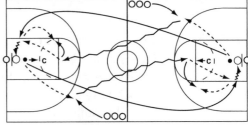

Diagram 23-E

Coaching Points:

1. to 5. - same as Drill #3.
6. Same as for Drill #3, except after coming to a jump stop under control, a bounce is made to the cutter.
7. Player making pass should follow his pass and slide to the lane side of the ball.
8. Concentration and correct form for the layup are essential. The shooter should jump upward and stay on the playing floor after the shot.

Drill #5 – Wing Jump Shot

Same as Drill #3, except middle man makes a direct pass to the cutter who comes to a jump shot under control and shoots the wing jump stop (Diagram F).

Diagram 23-F

Coaching Points:

1. to 5. - same as Drill #3.
6. Same as Drill #3, except a direct pass is made to the man cutting to the basket.
7. Player on the wing should catch the pass under control, come to a jump stop and take the jump shot under control.

Drill #6 – Return to Foul Line

Same as Drill #5, except the wing man returns the ball to the middle man as he slides to the elbow following his pass. The middle man should be ready to take the jump shot upon receiving the return pass as shown in Diagram F.

Coaching Points:

1. to 6. - same as Drill #5.
7. Same as Drill #5, except the wing player returns the ball to the middle man for the jump shot.
8. The middle man should slide along the foul line following his pass and be ready for the return pass for the jump shot.

Comments:

These drills are shown being run so that the outlet is to the right and the dribble up the middle should be with the left hand. Also, all the shots will be taken on the right side of the floor. For best results the drills should be run the opposite direction on alternate days (see Diagram G), which would then have the outlet to the left and the dribble up the middle with the right hand. The shooting would then be from the left side of the floor. This drill can be run in about 6 minutes of practice time and serves a number of purposes, including conditioning. This drill, like any other, is only beneficial if a good effort is put forth with attention to fundamentals and details during the execution.

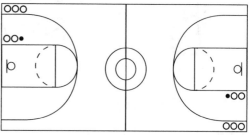

Diagram 23-G

Coaching Cues:

Emphasize quick, accurate passes, two hand catches, proper footwork, and basic shooting fundamentals. Go at top speed under control.

Coach:

Gary Miller wrote this article for the *Basketball Bulletin* after he was an assistant coach for Gettysburg College (PA).

Three-Man Weave
Shooting Drill

Purpose:

Teach players to pass, catch, and shoot on the move as they are being conditioned to play full-court basketball.

Description:

Players run three-man weave and three shots are taken at each end of the floor during a timed period, with a predetermined number of made baskets as a goal. See Diagram A for sequence.

Diagram 24-A

1. 3-man weave up – 2nd pass goes for a layup and gets own rebound.

2. Two players then go to passes for shots from baseline feeders.

3. Passer along with layup shooter repeat 3 man weave to other basket (jump shooters move to baseline with ball).

4. One layup and two jump shots at each end.

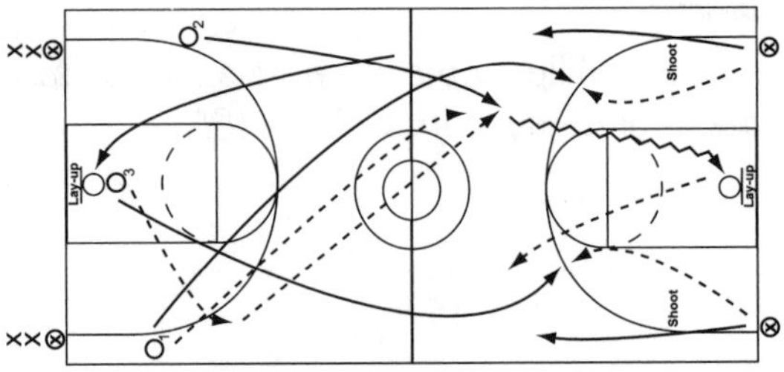

Coaching Cues:

Players focus on proper techniques of passing, catching, and shooting while running the floor at top speed under control.

Coach:

Bob Bender coaches the University of Washington Huskies in the Pacific-Ten Conference. He is noted for teaching balanced offense and defense and motion offense fundamentals.

Fundamental Drills
(Summer '80 Basketball Bulletin)

Purpose:

Teach players offensive and defensive fundamental skills to maximize development.

Description:

In twenty-nine years of coaching, I have never had a player who had a knee operation or a broken bone and yet I believe in having teams that play hard-nosed basketball on both ends of the court.

My practice sessions are never over two hours long and sometimes shorter. Sunday practices occur only for a Monday game. A typical practice includes the following drills stressing various fundamentals of this great game of basketball:

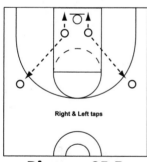
Shooting to 100

Diagram 25-A

- ◆ 10 minutes free shooting while waiting for all players to arrive on the court.
- ◆ 5 games of shooting to 100 from three different areas of the floor (see Diagram A); shooting to 100; players must make a long shot to start and endlongs 10 pts. each; all layins count 5 pts. after first long shot is made.

Right & Left taps

Diagram 25-B

- ◆ 20-20-10-10 rebounding drill with partner (Diagram B). 20 taps right-handed off backboard; 20 taps left-handed; 10 two-handed taps; 10 rebounds with ball overhead; outlet pass to partner.
- ◆ Free throws.
- ◆ Hop, step, and jump – I do not believe in stretching exercises or running bleachers (Diagram C). Player tosses ball on backboard and in one continuous motion, takes one hop landing on one foot in the lane to catch the ball on the other side with a jump stop.

Hop, Step, & Jump

Diagram 25-C

- ◆ 3 dribble - 2 dribble -1 dribble -no dribble- full court layup with partner as trailer stresses rebounding, lob pass and support of play as well as conditioning.

- Six station passing and layup drill with no dribbling (Diagram D). This is a continuous motion drill of no dribbling – all chest passes around the outside perimeter of the court. Each player has own ball and he passes the ball to a station, and receives it back.

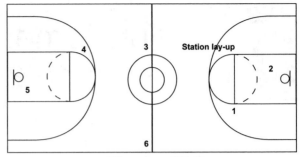

Diagram 25-D

   1 and 4 – set up for handoff for layup.

   2 and 5 – retrieve layup and make outlet pass.

   3 and 6 – stationed for passing and to keep players on outside perimeter.

- Reverse, crossover and reverse movements to the basket. Diagram E (1), (2), and (3).

- Reverse. Diagram E (1). 2 receives pass from 3 and reverses pivot, drops ball with outside hand and drives to the hoop. 3 trails, retrieves layup, makes outlet pass to 2 who has been continuing through on outside perimeter of court and then fills on line. 2 then passes to 3 who is near midcourt and then fills into that position with 2 moving into the line.

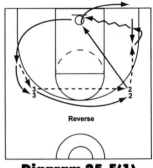

Reverse

Diagram 25-E(1)

- Reverse and Cross-over. Diagram E (2). Same as reverse, except 2 steps across his body with his outside foot and moves ball to the inside hand to dribble and go for the basket.

- Reverse, Cross-over and Reverse. Diagram E (3). Same as reverse and cross-over except 2 reverses on his drive towards the basket along the side of the key.

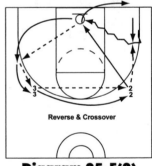

Reverse & Crossover

Diagram 25-E(2)

- Half-court fast break – 3-on-2.

- 1-on-1.

- 2-on-2.

- 4-on-4 – all three drills show offensive and defensive positioning.

- Free throws.

- Break.

- Jack-in-box (Diagram F). With over 5 players, two must be inside the circle and the outside players have only one foot on the circle. To get out of the middle, you must touch the ball in the player's hand, touch

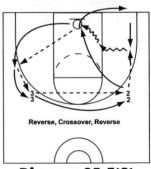

Reverse, Crossover, Reverse

Diagram 25-E(3)

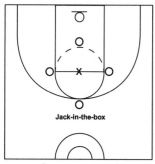

Jack-in-the-box

Diagram 25-F

or intercept a pass or when a player makes a bad pass which causes the outside man to move one of his feet from the circle.

The last forty minutes of practice is spent on team offensive and defensive patterns as well as special situation plays. With these drills stressed daily, I can recruit local players and develop these young men so that they can compete and win against teams that recruit nationally.

Coaching Cues:

Focus on correct executions of this fundamental skill package that is used daily.

Coach:

Hugh Thimlar coached twelve years in Indiana at the high school level and twenty years at Edison Community College in Fort Myers (FL). His teams were noted for their success in overachieving, largely with unrecruited players.

5-Ball Drill

Purpose:

Teach players to run the court (condition) while passing, catching, shooting and reaching a team goal.

Description:

The basic drill setup and organization is shown in Diagram A with five balls used, one at each basket.

Set scoreboard clock at 5 minutes.

Count made hoops. Potential of 3 points each trip, one for each basket made. Subtract 1 point for layup missed. Player in middle controls the pace by how fast he runs the court. Minimum of nine players, up to fifteen; dribble only to avoid traveling.

Three player pass and return pass to layup, bounce off baseline jumpshot (minimum shot is 12 ft.). Except for layup, rebound own shot, pass ball to wing, go to different line.

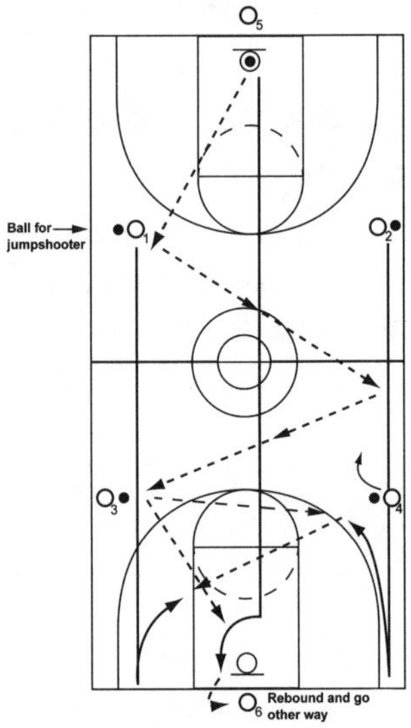

Diagram 26-A

Set realistic goal – if you don't succeed, run drill again.

Note: wings can cross under instead of bouncing off baseline – receive pass from that side instead of cross court pass.

Coaching Cues:

Focus on passing, catching, shooting and communication skills and principles. Be quick, but don't hurry – top speed under control. Players on wings fill lanes as passers, bounce off baseline for jump shot (or cross over for jump shot), rebound own shot, pass ball to new wing player and go to back of line on opposite wing. You may rotate middle lane ballhandler.

Coach:

Dennie Bridges has been the athletic director and basketball coach at Illinois Wesleyan for 32 years. During his tenure he has achieved 16 conference championships, 17 trips to NAIA or NCAA III national tournaments, and leads all active NCAA III coaches with 587 wins.

Freethrow
Conditioning Drill

Purpose:

Practice free throw shooting in game-like situations where fatigue is a factor.

Description:

The drill can be run for however long you wish. Suggest 4½ minutes, sounding the horn every 30 seconds. This allows 30 seconds for a water break at the end.

You will have three players to a basket – shooter, rebounder, and a runner.

The runner can either do sprints, full-court ballhandling drills, or full-court defensive slides. Emphasize to your runner to really work on whatever phase he is performing. He should be working at game speed.

At the sound of the horn the runner immediately goes to the free throw line. The shooter becomes the rebounder and the rebounder becomes the runner.

The shooter shoots as many free throws as he can in 30 seconds in his normal shooting routine, not rushing his shot.

A manager will chart the player's makes and misses. Diagram A shows the drill sequence.

Note: Stress the importance of making the first shot after being the runner. Overcoming the fatigue and scoring is the main goal of the drill.

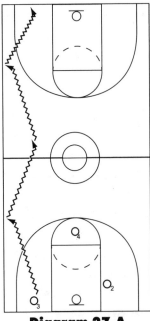

Diagram 27-A

Coaching Cues:

Work on your skills at game speed. Your first free throw is critical – perform your ritual and score. Get in your groove – shoot the same way each time.

Coach:

Tony Barone is now head coach of the Texas A&M Aggies, after a successful stint at Creighton University (NE).

Pressure Free Throws Drill

Purpose:

Teach players to shoot free throws in all competition situations that occur in a game.

Description:

Use this drill in practice at least twice per day for a five minute period. Players are placed in groups of 2 or 3 to a basket (prefer pairs, if enough baskets). Coach gathers squad, gives them emphasis and goal for the day. Examples of each are:

Emphasis

1. believe it will go in (no negatives)
2. same spot each time (alignment)
3. use same ritual (deep breath and finger on air hole)
4. follow through (until ball hits net)

Goals

1. consecutive made FT in your group – row 4, 5, 6, 7, or 8
2. FT situation – shoot one, shoot one and bonus if made (1-on-1), shoot 2, shoot 3
3. net FT – only count those that go through net without hitting rim (make 4, 5, or 6 – not consecutive
4. eyes closed – make 2 of 3 individually (partner gives feedback)

Groups must meet goal before getting a water break. Consequences of not meeting goal – 5 situps, or 5 pushups.

Coaching Cues:

Pick emphasis and goal for the day. Insist on gamelike approach – confident concentration.

Coach:

Jerry Krause has been coaching basketball for 33 years – high school (5) and college (28).

2-Lane Fast Break Buildup Drill

DRILL 29

Purpose:

Teach players to handle the ball (pass, catch, dribble, and score) on the two lane (2-on-0, 2-on-1) fast break completion.

Description:

Two lines at halfcourt 15 - 18 feet apart with a ball. This drill may be run at both ends of the floor simultaneously. The sequence is shown in Diagrams A, B, and C. A defender may be added to buildup from 2-on-0 to a 2-on-1 situation.

Diagram A shows the 2-0 (two-lane) fast break completion. In Diagram B, shooter 2 scores layup, sprints to freeline extended and calls outlet. 1 inbounds layup, calls ball and zips a quick pass to 2. In Diagram C, drill begins again as 2 passes to next player in line on his side of court.

Coaching Cues:

Start near halfcourt line, watch spacing (15-18 ft.). Pass and catch properly to score – crisp passes.

Coach:

John MacLeod heads the basketball program at Notre Dame University. Coach MacLeod has also coached at the professional level with the Phoenix Suns and formerly in college at the University of Oklahoma. He is noted for his emphasis on fast break basketball.

Diagram 29-A

Diagram 29-B

Diagram 29-C

Eleven Man
Fast Break Drill

Purpose:

Teach players offensive fast break position, ballhandling and shooting, disadvantage defense in fast break situations, and offense/defensive rebounding from the fast break. This is an excellent full-court conditioning drill.

Description:

The minimum number of players for the drill is eleven. To start the drill, three players from team "A" attack 3 on 2 against the "B" team, as shown in Diagram A. Play continues until team A scores or team B gains possession. Offensive team receives normal scoring points, plus two points if fouled in the act of shooting. A coach at each end of the floor calls fouls and determines scores (kept on the scoreboard). On a score,

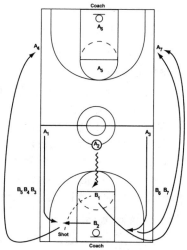

Diagram 30-A

a defender from team B inbounds the ball. That B player passes to one of the two new B outlet players on the inbound pass (score) or on an outlet pass (miss/rebound). These three B team players then attack the A defenders (3 on 2) at the other end of the court.

The remaining B defender is joined by another B player from the sideline for the next series of defense. Players from each team circle back up the sidelines to reenter play on the next series.

Coaching Cues:

Coaches should emphasize their specific offensive and defensive fast break strategies. Offensive players should try to get a good shot with a minimum number of dribbles and passes. Crash the boards on offense. Fast break defenders should protect the basket, stop the ball, block out on shots, and go to the ball. The drill may be run for a period of time or to a predetermined score.

Coach:

Dave Frohman and Chris Sload coach at Dickinson College. Frohman is in his 9th year as head coach, where his teams have won championships in 1992 and 1997, and led the nation in 3-point FG percent in 1992. He is also an active member of the NABC Research Committee and has spent 24 years in the coaching profession, also at Xavier, Westminster (PA), and Milan (IN) high school. Sload is in his third year as an assistant with the Red Devils.

Sooner 4-Minute Layup Drill

Purpose:

Teach players to pass, catch, shoot, and condition on the full court as they strive for a team goal.

Description:

The basic drill organization and movement is shown in Diagram A.

Drill sets up with a line of shooters under each basket and a passer at each of the elbows.

As the drill begins, the first player in line passes to the nearest elbow, this pass is returned to the shooter via a bounce pass thrown out in front of the shooter as he heads towards the opposite goal.

Shooter then passes to the next elbow, cuts hard to the basket, receives a drop-off bounce pass and shoots the layup.

Next shooter in line takes the ball from the net and does the same routine going the other way.

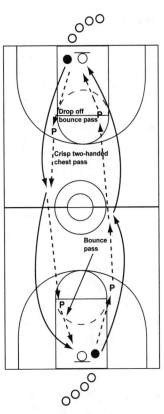

Diagram 31-A

Coaching Cues:

♦ Keep the ball off the floor; there should be no dribbles.

♦ Switch passers at the 2-minute mark.

♦ Set a goal of between 80-90 makes; 90 is very good!

Coach:

Kelvin Sampson, successful head coach of the Oklahoma Sooners, after a successful stint at Washington State University. He was also an assistant at Michigan State and head coach of Montana Tech. His teams are noted for their tenacious defense and competitiveness.

Wheel Fast Break

Purpose:

Teach players an organized fast break system.

Description:

Start players on defense and run a 5-on-0 fast break from made and missed FG and FT situations. Progress to 5-on-2, 3 and 4, following the basic rules.

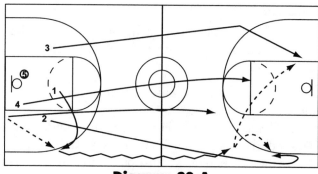

Diagram 32-A

Wheel Fast Break Options (made or missed baskets and free throws)

Wheel Fast break (see Diagram A). First possible player will fly to the ball-side corner to flatten the defense and step to meet the pass. Outlet player should push the ball up the court hard, pass to spot-up corner shooter or skip pass to open cutter, then look to cut to the basket. Rebounder will follow up the ball side for the open outside elbow jump shot, pass inside, or ready to start the FLEX.

Wheel Fast break (see Diagram B). Pass-cut options: should drive the defense back to open low post area for diagonal cutter and trailing rebounder. ALL PLAYERS SHOULD KNOW ALL POSITIONS FOR THE WHEEL!!

Wheel fastbreak

Secondary Wheel Fast break (see Diagram C). Trailer can shoot the jumper, pass inside, or reverse the ball to start the FLEX.

Diagram 32-B

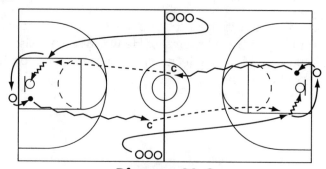

Diagram 32-C

Diagram 32-D

Flex Options (see Diagram D). Strongside corner player should cut baseline off low post screen. Strongside passer should PICK THE PICKER on ball reversal.

FLEX (see Diagram E). Work the FLEX from side to side if not open on the first ball reversal.

Coaching Cues:

All fast break fundamentals can be emphasized as the fast break is drilled from all situations. Push the ball up the court on all situations. Advance the ball up the sideline. On corner overplay, backcut to the basket. On outlet player traps use the #4 player as an outlet to relieve pressure.

Diagram 32-E

Coach:

Jerry Hueser was the longtime coach at the University of Nebraska-Kearney, where he became a coaching legend in the NAIA and NCAA II. His teams were noted for their fast break style of play.

DRILL
33

Middle 1-on-1

Purpose:

Teach players to practice 1-on-1 offensive skills in quick, gamelike competitive situations.

Description:

Players arranged in offensive and defensive pairs, one pair per basket with extra players in the center jump circle area (middle). See Diagram A. As each pair has a one-on-one competition the players in the middle are working on an offensive ballhandling or defensive footwork skill. 1-on-1 rules are to start with a live ball, must face the basket, two dribble limit, and make it – take it (player who scores keeps the ball). The winner is the first player to three baskets, with loser replacing a teammate in the middle. Competition drill lasts for 5 - 7 minutes.

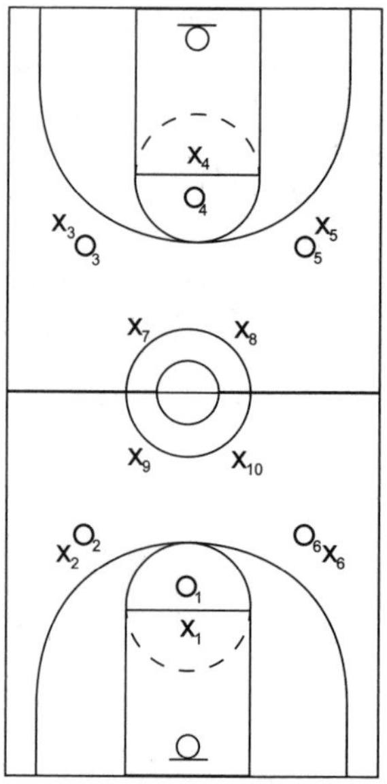

Coaching Cues:

Coaches should focus on 1-on-1 offensive and defensive principles, such as

Diagram 33-A

- ♦ offense – triple threat, face basket, attack defender's front foot, read the defense, make quick straight line drive moves, follow your shot.
- ♦ defense – active hands and feet, stay in stance, take away opponent's strength, act – don't react, block out on each shot, pressure each shot without fouling.

Coach:

Heather Kirk, assistant women's coach at the United States Military Academy at West Point.

DRILL

34

Quickness Drills
Summer '84 Basketball Bulletin

Purpose:

Develop basketball skill-related quickness with circuit training stations.

Description:

We pride ourselves on pressure defense all over the floor. I think we are fortunate in the fact that we can recruit quickness, where as many times in high school a coach has to work with the talent he has. Being a coach over the past twenty years, seven in high school and thirteen in college, I have tried all of the different conditioning programs, such as running the track for distance and sprints, also running stadium stairs, golf courses, cross country, gym line drills, etc. I have found that sometimes you end up with a better track team than basketball team. We as coaches are always taking ideas from different sports and other basketball coaches, therefore, our game runs in fads as far as offenses and defenses are concerned. What we all want are good athletes with great attitudes and then go to work from there.

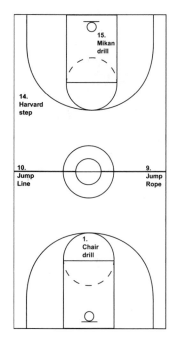
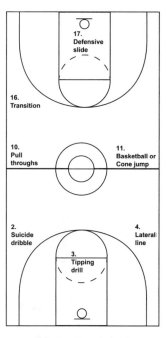
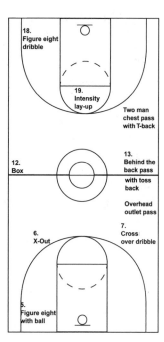

Diagram 34-A

Our way for developing quickness is not the only way, it is just one of the many ways. I hope you get some ideas from my discussion that you might want to add to your program or might motivate you to always be looking for something new and interesting for your athletes.

We set up the gym with anywhere from 14-19 stations that we call quickness stations (see Diagram A). In the rotation design we have developed, a player gets at each station and the drill is run for 30 seconds with 30 seconds to change stations. The fact we have basketballs incorporated into the drills takes away from the boredom. Also at each station there is a pencil and paper for the players to record his or her scores. Each drill has an excellent or good rating on the number of times the exercise is completed in the 30 second time allotment. Therefore, in 15 to 19 minutes you can get quickness, conditioning, ballhandling, defensive foot work and competition all done at the same time; while no one is standing around.

Coaching Cues:

Emphasis is placed on proper execution of all skills at top speed. Each rotation is one minute (30 sec. station and 30 sec. change periods). Design the circuit to fit your situation.

Coach:

Under the helm of Ralph Underhill in the 1980s, Wright State appeared in five NCAA II tournaments, winning the national title in 1983 when Ralph was selected as NABC Coach of the Year.

Defensive Slide:

Don't cross feet

1. Pass to Toss Back from one foul line corner.
2. React to return pass from Toss Backand slide to opposite corner. Repeat. Corner slides.

30 seconds. Excellent – 28+, Good – 22-27, Fair – 15-21

Behind-the-back Wrap – Two Hands

Side to Toss Back

1. Wrap the ball behind the back to the Toss Back.
2. Catch ball off Toss Back with two hands and repeat.

30 seconds. Excellent – 40+, Good – 33-39, Fair – 25-32

Defensive slide

Behind the back wrap – two hands

Behind-the-back Wrap –One Hand

Basketball Jump   **Line Jump**

Rebound Drill

Mikan Drill   **Jump Rope**

Behind-the-back Wrap – One Hand

Side to Toss Back

1. Wrap the ball behind the back to the Toss Back.
2. Catch ball off Toss Back with throwing hand and repeat.

30 seconds. Excellent – 35+, Good 28-34, Fair 20-27

Basketball Jump

Great for knee and ankle strength and quickness.

30 seconds. Excellent – 5+, Good – 45-54, Fair – 30-44

Line Jump

Feet together. Jump the line without touch it, back and forth.

30 seconds. Excellent – 120+, Good – 105-119, Fair – 90-104

Rebound Drill

1. Hands overhead. Strong pass to Toss Back.
2. Quick jump to rebound and sink basket. Baskets per minute: Excellent – 14+, Good – 10-13, Fair 6-9

Mikan Drill

Continuous Layups. Right hand layup, grab ball, left hand layup, grab ball and alternate.

30 seconds. Excellent – 20+, Good – 15-19, Fair 10-14

Jump Rope

Fine training for foot mobility.

60 seconds. Excellent – 140+, Good – 125-139, Fair – 100-124

Cross-over Dribble

Three cones at 3' intervals. Start 3' before cone #1. left hand dribble, switch to right hand at cone #1, to left at cone #2, and alternate down and back. Excellent to complete this drill – 7-9 seconds, Good – 10-12 seconds, Fair – 13-15 seconds.

Lateral Line

Stay down; kick off with outside leg. Drive sideways to foul line from top of key; return.

30 seconds. Excellent – 37+, Good – 30-36, Fair – 25-29

Suicide Dribble

Right hand dribble out; left hand back; stay within lines. Baseline to free throw and return. Baseline to halfcourt and return. Excellent – 10 seconds, Good – 13-15 seconds, Fair – 1-19 seconds.

X-out

Start right corner. Right hand dribble – layup – right hand dribble to left corner. Then left hand return dribble. 30 second layup count. Excellent – 7+, Good – 5-6, Fair 3-4

Jab Step

Feed to Toss Back, quick jab step fake, react catch from Toss Back, and quick shot release. No time. Work on quick moves.

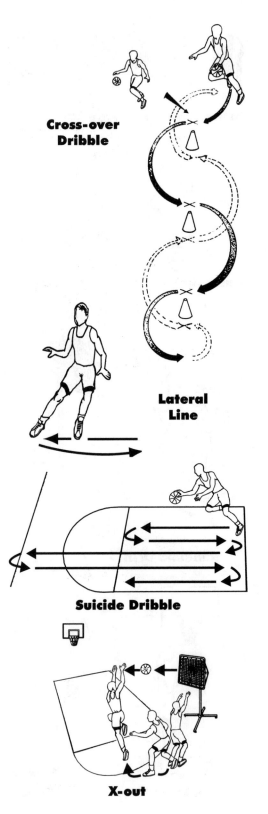

Cross-over Dribble

Lateral Line

Suicide Dribble

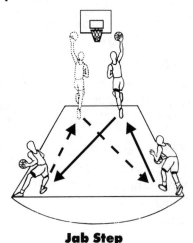

Jab Step

X-out

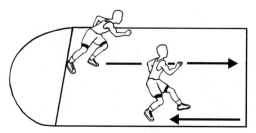

Transition

Transition

Keep low.

1. From foul line dig for baseline.
2. BACKUP drive to free throw line. Repeat.

30 seconds. Excellent – 14+, Good – 10-13, Fair – 7-9

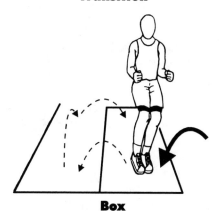

Box

Box

Feet together. Skip the lines. Face forward. From outside box, jump to square one, two three, four, one, etc. 60 seconds. Excellent – 80+, Good – 60-79, Fair – 50-59

Continuity Outlet

Bounce ball off backboard, grab, outlet to Toss Back for react pass at foul line, dribble to repeat. 30 seconds. Excellent – 6+, Good – 4-5, Fair – 2-3

Continuity Outlet

Intensity Layup

Pass to Toss Back from top of key. Catch the ball in stride and layup. Grab ball and dribble to top of key. 30 second layup count. Excellent – 7+, Good – 5-6, Fair –3-4

Harvard Step

Body low. Step up one step and back down and repeat. 30 seconds. Excellent – 45+, Good – 37-44, Fair – 30-36

Figure Eight Speed Dribble

Start the drill in either with either the right or left hand, start dribbling in and out between your legs in a figure eight manner. Start slowly and keep the ball as low as possible at all times. Gradually pick up speed after you begin to master the drill. There is no time limit to the drill although 20 times around in a minute is excellent, 10 in 30 seconds.

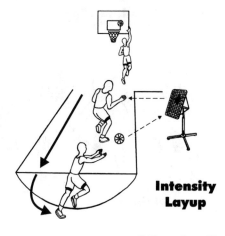

Intensity Layup

Blurr

Start the drill with the legs about shoulder width apart. One hand will be on the ball in front of the legs and the other hand will be on the ball in the back of the legs as shown. Then flip the ball in the air and reverse the position of your hands. Catch the ball in the fingertips and try to go as fast as you can for 30 seconds. The ball will seem to sit between your legs if executed properly. Excellent – 80-100, Good – 60-80, Fair – 40-60

Straddle Flip

Start with the legs shoulder width apart witht the knees bent. Hands in front holding the basketball. Let go of the ball or flip it very slightly up in the air between your legs. Now bring your hands to the back of your legs and catch the ball before it hits the ground. Now flip the ball again in the air and bring your hands back to the front as quick as you can. Drill as fast as you can without dropping the ball. Drill is done for 30 seconds. Excellent – 90+, Good – 60-80, Fair – 40-60

Rhythm

Take the ball around the right leg. Grab the ball with the left hand in front, right hand in back. Drop the ball. Quickly reverse hands and catch the ball after one bounce. Move the ball back to start around left leg. Opposite drill: start with the ball in the left hand. Drill is done for 30 seconds. Excellent – 33-40, Good – 21-32, Fair – 10-20

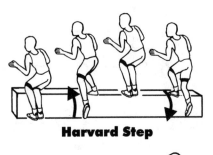

Harvard Step

Figure Eight Speed Dribble

Blurr

Straddle Flip

Rhythm

The **NABC** Drill Book

Double Leg/Single Leg

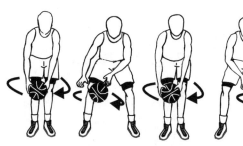

Double Leg/Single Leg

Take the ball behind the legs and around to the front. When the ball reaches the right hand spread your legs and take the ball around the right leg only. Then close your legs and take the ball once around both legs, then open your les and take the ball around your left leg once then back to two legs again. The ball always moves in the same direction.

Opposite drill: start the ball in the left hand.

Drill is done for 30 seconds.

Excellent – 50-70, Good – 35-50, Fair – 25-35

Around the Waist

Around the Waist

Take the ball in the right hand and take it behind your back and catch it with your left hand and in one continuous motion bring the ball around to the front to your right hand. Do the drill continuously for 30 seconds as fast as possible. Drill is then done by starting with the ball in the left hand.

Fair – 25-35, Good – 35-50, Excellent – 55-70

Around the Head

Around the Head

Place the ball in the right hand and with your shoulders back take the ball behind your head and catch it with your left hand and bring it around to the front to your right hand in a continuous motion.

Opposite drill: start with the ball in the left hand. Drill is done for 30 seconds.

Fair – 30-40, Good – 40-50, Excellent – 55-75

Head, Waist & Leg Rhythm Drill

Figure Eight From the Back

Start with the ball in the right hand. Take it between your legs to your left hand. Then with the ball in the left hand take it behind your left leg and between your legs to your right hand. Continue drill for 30 seconds.

Opposite drill is figure eight from the front which takes the ball right and left hand through the front of your legs.

Excellent – 75-85, Good – 50-65, Fair – 30-45

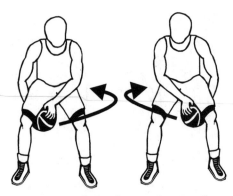

Figure Eight from the Back

Figure Eight With One Bounce

Start with the legs shoulder width and the knees bent. With the ball in the right hand bounce it between your legs and catch it with your left hand behind your legs then with the ball in the left hand bring it around to the front and bounce it between your legs and catch it with your right hand.

Opposite drill: take the ball behind the legs and bounce it to the front right and left hand.

Excellent – 40-50, Good – 30-40, Fair – 20-30

Figure Eight with One Bounce

Intensity Drills
Spring '91 Basketball Bulletin

Purpose:

Teach players to increase intensity and effort during practices and games by specific drills.

Description:

The following drills are designed to increase intensity and effort during practice and games. As coaches, sometimes our toughest job is to get our players to under-stand how to play harder and with more intensity. We put a lot of emphasis on playing hard and with intensity in all of our drill work. The purpose of any drill is to improve individual or team performance. This can only be accomplished through intensity and a sincere effort on the individual's part. Encourage your players to do more and they will. Remember, if you want your players to be hard workers and play with intensity then so must you.

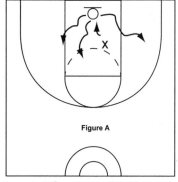

Figure A

Diagram 35-A

Intensity Shooting Drill (see Diagram A)

The main goal in this drill is to attempt and make as many shots in one minute as possible. Always start under the basket with a layup or similar easy shot. After the ball comes through the net you take **two** hard dribbles away from the basket in any direction. Turn, square up, shoot, concentrating on each shot. After the shot you bust your tail to get the rebound then repeat for one minute. Your goal is to make 10-12 shots before the coach blows the whistle. Dribble in all directions. Go as hard as possible. Concentrate. Square up and follow through.

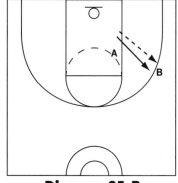

Diagram 35-B

Offense-Defense Shooting Drill (see Diagram B)

The main goal in this shooting drill is to make five shots before your opponent does. Both players will be applying heavy defensive pressure. Drill in-volves two players and one ball. Player A should position himself on the block, Player B should be about 15-17 feet away on the wing. Player A starts the drill by passing the ball to B. Player A then sprints out and tries to block B's shot. Player B is in ready-to-shoot position as he catches the ball; he then shoots it as quickly as he can. After he shoots the ball he rebounds the ball and passes the ball back to player A from the block. Player A has replaced B and B has replaced A. The passer becomes the shooter and the shooter becomes the passer. You can structure this drill where the shooter catches the ball and shoots quickly or where the shooter is allowed one or two dribbles. This is a high-intensity drill. You may want to go to 3 or 4 baskets.

Four-Minute Layup Drill (see Diagram C)

The main objective in this drill is to make (as a team) 80-85 layups either right-handed or left-handed in four minutes. Players A, B, C and D are on the passing lanes. Players E and F are in the right-hand layup position. As the coach blows the whistle the clock starts. It can be a stop watch or the game clock. Player E passes to A and F passes to D. Players E and F are sprinting as hard as they can. Players A and D catch the ball then pivot on their inside foot and pass ahead to E and F. After E and F receive the pass, they then execute a two-hand chest pass to B or C. Players B and C step and receive the ball then execute a drop step bounce pass to E and F for a layup. Remember, E and F are sprinting the whole way.

It is important to make good passes. This cannot be emphasized enough. After the shooters make their layups they go to the end of their respective lines. The next person in line should be ready to get the ball out of the net and go. Both lines are going simultaneously. At the 2-minute mark the coach blows his whistle and four new players replace the four existing players in the passing lane.

Short 17/Short 21 (Conditioning Drill) (see Diagram D)

In this drill, each player starts on one sideline and must touch the sidelines 17 times in one minute. This can be increased to 21 times in a minute, if desired. Each player must **touch** each line with either his hand or his foot, whichever the coach requires. If all players do not make the required number under one minute, then everyone must repeat the drill.

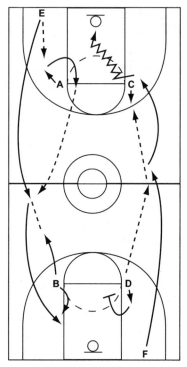

Diagram 35-C

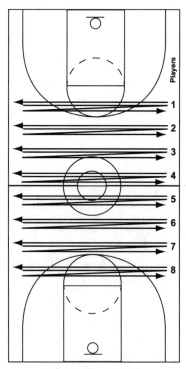

Diagram 35-D

Foot Agility Drill (see Diagram E)

This is an adaptation of the old "quarterback" foot quickness drill. This drill can be used to improve foot quickness and agility (especially good for big men). The spots may be used for various foot quickness variations.

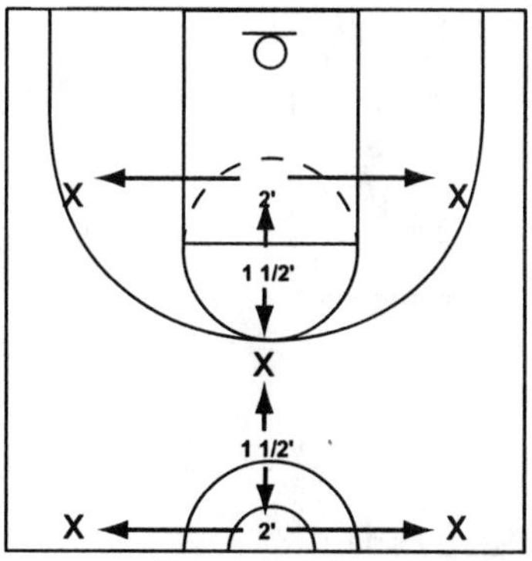

Spots

Shoot a designated move, shot and spot. Earn the "spot" by making the established number of field goals from that distance. Move to a new "spot."

Diagram 35-E

Coaching Cues:

Focus on proper execution at top speed – do it right and do it quickly.

Coach:

Kelvin Sampson is head coach of the Oklahoma University Sooners, and is presently serving on the NABC Board of Directors. His teams are noted for their intensity.

Three-Man Full Court Continuous Layups

Purpose:

Teach players to rebound, outlet the ball, run the court, and score a fast break layup in two passes.

Description:

Diagram A shows the first half of a sequence starting on one baseline – rebounder in the middle.

- 3 lines at end of court
- post players in the middle line
- perimeter players in outside lines
- post player in the middle starts drill
- outlet ball to perimeter player who steps out to right wing
- perimeter player catches outlet then starts downcourt
- after 1 dribble, player throws long pass to other perimeter player on the left side of the court
- left perimeter player makes layup

The return trip back to the starting baseline is shown in Diagram B and described below.

- post player hustles down the middle of the court to get the ball out of the net
- right side perimeter player hustles down the court and gets both feet in the middle of the key area
- post player takes ball out of bounds and makes the outlet again
- perimeter player who made the layup now becomes the outlet
- perimeter player in the key area becomes recipient of the long pass for the layup
- both the post player and the outlet man must cross half court before the second layup is made
- the next post player in line gets the ball out of the net to continue the drill
- goal for the drill is to make 40 layups in 3 minutes.

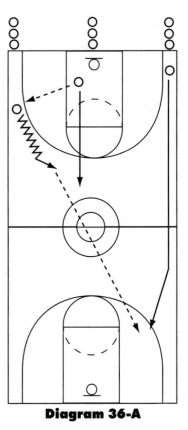

Diagram 36-A

The **NABC** Drill Book

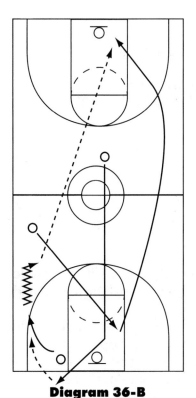

Diagram 36-B

Coaching Cues:

Start drill with a rebound from a backboard toss. Check passing and catching fundamentals – go at top speed under control. Complete the fast break with a <u>score</u>.

Coach:

Sherman Dillard became the new head coach at James Madison in 1997, after four years at Indiana State University. He assisted Lefty Driesell at Maryland from 1979-85, Lou Companelli at California from 1985-88, and Bobby Cremins at Georgia Tech from 1988-94. Dillard, the second-leading scorer in JMU history is a magna cum laude graduate of JMU.

Wraparound Out-of-Bounds Series

Purpose:

Teach players on offensive with common elements for side and under out-of-bounds situations.

Description:

The basic alignment is a "tight box" as shown in Diagram A, with two inside players O_4 and O_5 on the ballside and two perimeter players away from the ball and a perimeter player taking the ball out-of-bounds.

Diagram C shows the under out-of-bounds sequence – backscreen for inside player 4, wraparound by perimeter player 1, wraparound by 2, pop back by 5 and 3 steps in after pass. If 3 passes to 2, 3 steps in and 5 screens away for 1 (see Diagram D). If 3 makes the entry pass to 5, 3 backscreens 2 and 4 makes a "muscle post" move (see Diagram E). If 5 passes to 1, Diagram F shows 5 screening for 3 after 3 backscreens for 2 as 4 posts up.

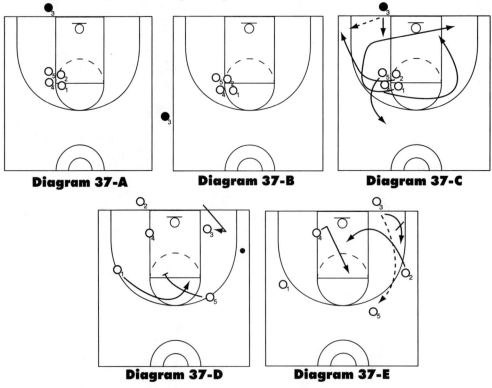

Diagram 37-A　　**Diagram 37-B**　　**Diagram 37-C**

Diagram 37-D　　**Diagram 37-E**

The side out-of-bounds series has the same elements as seen in Diagram G: 2 backscreens 4, 1 wraparound 5, 2 wraparound 5, and 5 pop out. In Diagram H, 3 passes to 2 which results in 4 posting up ballside and 5 backscreening for 3. If 3 makes the entry pass to 5, 2 backscreens 3, 4 steps in, 5 swings to 1 and screens for screener 2(see Diagram I).

Coaching Cues:

Simplify out-of-bounds plays by creating common elements in all situations. For example, this series has backscreens, wrap around cuts, popout cuts, and screen the screener situations. Design them and drill them so they are effective against all types of defenses.

Coach:

Bobby Cremins has been at Georgia Tech since 1981, after stints at Point Park (PA), South Carolina and Appalachian State. His 1989-90 team went to the NCAA I Final Four and garnered him National Coach of the Year honors. Cremins was assistant coach for the 1996 Olympic Gold Medal Medalist USA basketball team.

Diagram 37-F

Diagram 37-G

Diagram 37-H

Diagram 37-H

Two-Ball
Rebounding Drill

Purpose:

Teach players to make a continuous effort to go for the ball when offensive rebounding; secondarily to blockout, rebound and outlet the ball on defense.

Description:

The drill involves 3-on-3 competition between offensive and defensive players and coach or manager as shooter/outlet receivers, as seen in Diagram A. The drill starts with the coach shooting a ball. If the defenders gain control, they outlet the ball to coach or man-

Diagram 38-A

ager; if offensive players capture ball, they try to score on the offensive rebound. As soon as the first ball is controlled, the manager shoots the second ball. Both groups rebound both shots. The drill continues until an offensive player rebounds and scores.

Coaching Cues:

Defenders – always make contact and go to the ball. Offensive rebounders – anticipate the rebound and go to an open spot. Pursue each rebound.

Coach:

George Karl is the head coach of the Seattle Supersonics where he has won over 300 games. He has won championships in the CBA and Real Madrid in Spain. Karl was an All-American guard under Dean Smith at North Carolina in 1973.

Moving Pairs Passing Drill

Purpose:

Teach offensive players the basics of spacing, passing, catching, moving without the ball, and moves with the ball (catch and face, pass or drive/pass).

Description:

Each pair of players has a ball and a basket plus court space (can go with two groups per basket). Player without the ball executes v-cuts to get open until the ball handler passes the ball with a one-hand push pass. Receiver always catches the ball with feet in the air, lands with a quick (jump) stop, pivots and faces the basket in triple threat position. The partners continue cutting, passing and catching, pivot and facing the basket as shown in Diagram A. Note possible options seen:

1. left hand pass, catch and face
2. pass and catch, penetrate drive and pass back
3. pass false, backdoor cut and pass
4. penetrate, slide away and pass
5. pass fake, V cut and flare cut
6. pass and catch, penetrate – slide away and pass.

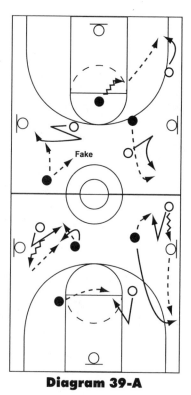

Diagram 39-A

Coaching Cues:

Pass with feet on the floor, catch with feet in the air, with the ball – pivot and face the basket with ball in triple threat. Maintain 15-18 ft. spacing.

Coach:

Jerry Krause has been NABC Research Committee chair for 30 years and has coached for 33 years, at secondary school (5 yrs.) and college level (28 yrs.).

DEFENSIVE
FUNDAMENTAL
DRILLS

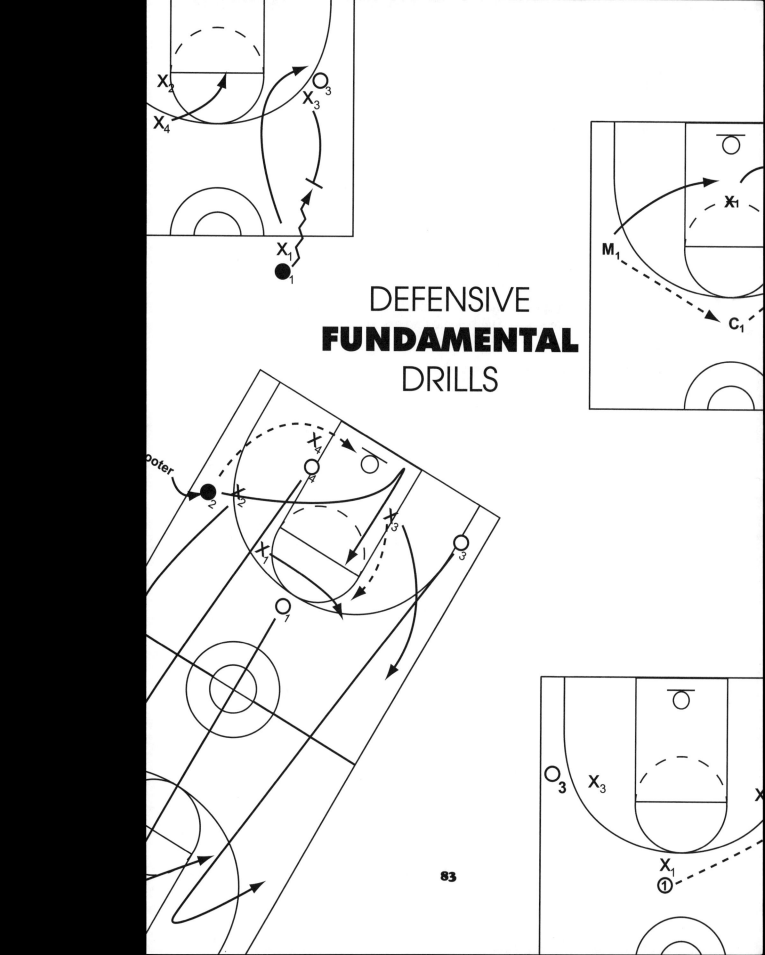

Stentz Drill

Purpose:

Defensive stance, feet-hands-head position, and individual defensive skills.

Description:

Coach facing team spread over court. Coach uses verbal commands to direct defensive players; players repeat verbal cue and execute movement.

Coaching Cues:

- ♦ big steps and direction – exaggerate the "reach" step defensive slide.
- ♦ jab-jab hands to either side both high and low to anticipate a pass deflection.
- ♦ chop steps – "machine gun" steps in place.
- ♦ closeout – on ball, contest shot, and block out imaginary offensive player.
- ♦ loose ball – dive on floor.
- ♦ take a charge – simulate contact and being knocked down on back (scramble up).

Coach:

Dr. Ron Righter, Head Coach, Clarion University, Clarion, PA. Former assistant at University of South California, Iowa, and Washington State. Specialty - offensive sets and counters, flex offense.

Y Drill

Purpose:

Teach defensive stance, starts, and steps.

Description:

Coach with ball facing team spread over court. (Figure A)Coach gives defensive verbal/signal commands for movement. The defensive slide movements can be "slow and perfect" or game speed. The options are:

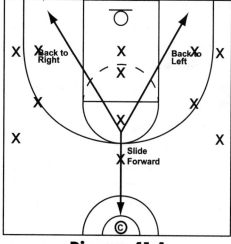

Diagram 41-A

- ◆ forward slide (signal-hitchhiker)
- ◆ diagonal back right or left (signal-point)
- ◆ side left or right (signal with ball)
- ◆ trace ball (coach move ball)
- ◆ dead ball (coach one bounce dribble)
- ◆ closeout (verbal command)
- ◆ toss ball to floor – loose ball

Coaching Cues:

- ◆ forward slide – slide with front foot first step
- ◆ diagonal slide – drop step and lead with foot in direction of movement
- ◆ trace ball – both hands on ball, stay in stance
- ◆ dead ball – swarm offensive player, trace ball
- ◆ closeout – sprint, get in stance and slide, contest shot, block out
- ◆ loose ball – all dive on floor, two-hand grab for ball while landing on chest, make imaginary pass and scramble up.

Coach:

Jerry Krause has been a basketball coach for 33 years – high school (5) and college (28).

Run – Glide – Run

Purpose:

Teach defensive player guarding the dribbler the necessary defensive skills needed when beaten on the dribble.

Description:

Place a offensive and defensive pair going 1-on-1 fullcourt. Switch offense and defense roles on the return trip.

Coaching Cues:

Whenever offense beats defender on the dribble the defender pivots and turns shoulders perpendicular to the dribbler's path. Defender gets low by "putting chest on knees" and takes at least two stride steps to catch up. When near dribbler, take one extra stride, pivot and lock up on dribble again in a low, wide stance.

Coach:

Jerry Tarkanian, now head coach at Fresno State (CA), made pressure defense famous with his famous UNLV teams.

DRILL 43

Vision Drill

Purpose:

Teach players the man-to-man defensive skill of maintaining vision on the ball and man, and other off-the-ball defensive skills.

Description:

- ♦ Coach handles the ball
- ♦ X_1 is in middle of lane on defense
- ♦ Offense starts in corner away from ball on weak side. Offense moves up to FT line extended (see Figure A) to make defense move also (see man and ball).
- ♦ Offense then cuts to weakside block (defense must move and adjust).
- ♦ Offense then flashes to high post. Defense must deny the flash (see Figure B).
- ♦ Offense then cuts back door then post up on block for 2-second count (Figure C).
- ♦ Defense plays back door cut then must front the post on ball side.
- ♦ Offense pops out to corner and defense must deny lead (see Figure D).
- ♦ Offense cuts back door, then clears out to weak side (see Figure E).

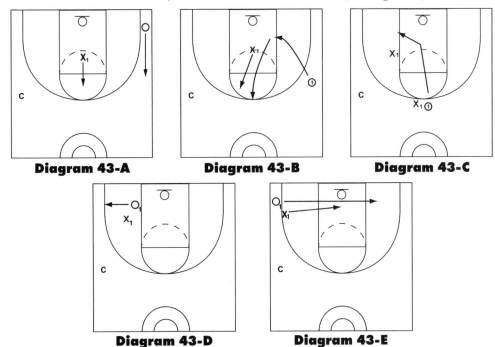

Diagram 43-A   **Diagram 43-B**   **Diagram 43-C**

Diagram 43-D   **Diagram 43-E**

◆ Defense plays back door cut, then stops middle of lane to play coach driving to basket (take the charge). (see Figure F)

Diagram 43-F

Coaching Cues:

The defender is exposed to nearly every defensive situation faced away from the ball during the drill sequence – all fundamentals can be evaluated.

Coach:

Steve Robinson is known as a coach whose players excel off and on the court. The head coach at Florida State recently spent two successful years at Tulsa (22-8, 24-10), and previously seven years as an assistant at Kansas University.

IBA Drill

(named after Hall of Fame Coach Henry "Hank" Iba of Oklahoma State University)

Purpose:

Teach players the team skills of help defense (take a charge), recover a loose ball (dive on the floor), and score in the lane (paint) with defensive contact.

Description:

In Figure A, X_1 is in defensive help position with ball at M_1 (manager). Ball is passed quickly to coach C_1 to O_1 who drives to basket. X_1 must get in dribbler O_1's path, take a charge and scramble to his feet. Coach C_1 immediately rolls ball anywhere in the frontcourt and X_1 must dive on the floor to retrieve ball with two hands while landing on chest, then passing back to coach before again scrambling back to feet (see Figure B). The final phase occurs when X_1 goes into the FT lane to receive a pass from coach and score through/over/around two managers with blocking dummies to create contact on X_1. X_1 must score, pass to coach and receive return pass until he has scored three times (see Figure C).

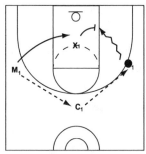

Diagram 44-A

Diagram 44-B

Coaching Cues:

- charge – move feet to get squarely in path of dribbler, get hands out of defense (put over groin area), and must be knocked down, scramble up.
- recover loose ball – both hands on ball, dive on chest, pass while down, scramble up.
- chin ball, score in traffic, expect and go through contact.

Diagram 44-C

Coach:

Eddie Sutton, Oklahoma State University coach, played for Iba at OSU and has coached at Kentucky, Arkansas, and Creighton University (NE).

DRILL 45

Approach – Contest – Scramble

Purpose:

Teach players to recognize and communicate defensive situations and teach the proper defensive techniques of approach, contest, help and scramble. To build defensive aggressiveness and toughness.

Description:

Figure A depicts the drill beginning with three offense players at three point FG line distance and three defenders under the basket and in the lane. Coach has a ball to start the drill with a pass to any offensive player. The rule requires each defender to take someone other than their matchup. For example, on the pass to 1, X_1 approaches 1, X_3 and X_2 closeout in a denial/help position to their offensive player (as shown in the diagram). If coach passes to an offensive player on the wing, as seen in Figure B, one defender approaches the ball, one approaches in a help position on the player on top, and the other defender takes a defensive position helpside guarding opposite wing.

Offensive players can catch and shoot, play 1-on-1, screen, penetrate and pass to get a good shot and score.

Diagram 45-A

Diagram 45-B

Coaching Cues:

Defense – communicate (ball, help), aggressively approach ball and help positions, help and recover, deny passes, flash cuts, guard screens, cover down, contest the shot and continue play to the defensive rebound.

Coach:

Larry Hunter, head coach of Ohio University, has an overall record of 447-169 (.726) in 21 seasons of coaching. At Wittenberg, his team won the NCAA III title in 1977, with four other Final Four appearances. His teams are always noted for their fundamentals.

Get on the Floor

Purpose:

Teach players to dive on the floor for a loose ball, recover the ball and pass from the floor to a teammate.

Description:

Players are grouped in pairs (see Figure A). Coach rolls ball on floor in front court – both players hustle to area of ball and dive on the floor for the ball. Player must grasp ball with both hands as they front dive on their chest. The player who gets the ball stays down on the floor with ball as his partner scrambles up to receive a pass and dribble drive (one

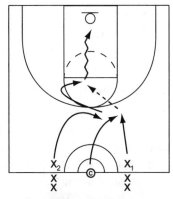

Diagram 46-A

dribble) for a layup. The passer must then scramble up and be at the basket for a follow in the event of a missed shot.

Coaching Cues:

Get on the floor for your team. Dive face down and grasp ball with both hands on your chest (use a volleyball dive). Pass while you are down (rules require). Score on the save and assume a miss.

Coach:

Jerry Krause has coached for 33 years at all levels of basketball.

Chesting Cutters – Odom

Diagram 47-A

Purpose:

Teach players to deny flash cuts into the FT lane and defend those cutters who receive the ball (1-on-1 defense).

Description:

Coach has the ball to start the drill in Figure A, where 1 makes a flash cut into the post area. X_1 denies the cut and "chests" the cutter in the FT lane and forces the offensive player into a less desirable area to receive the ball and then defend 1-on-1 facing the basket. The objective is to force the cutter outside – on top or to short corner.

Coaching Cues:

Defender forms a flat triangle with ball and offensive player, see man and ball, stay in stance, be alert and ready, chest cutter in the lane, deny the pass inside the lane.

Coach:

Dave Odom is a successful coach at Wake Forest University, where his teams are perennial conference title contenders and a regular NCAA I tournament selection.

1-on-1 Fullcourt

Purpose:

Teach defensive players the skills of defending a ballhandler – live ball, dribbler, and offensive player with the dead ball.

Description:

Using only half the court (divide the court with a line through the two end baskets), pair up an offensive player with the ball and a defender on the full court. Drill begins with a live ball situation with defender trying to prevent the dribble drive. The offensive player then advances ball on the dribble in a zigzag action and tries to beat the defender. Defender maintains ball-you-basket relationship with defensive sliding or running technique until near the far baseline, when the dribbler picks up the ball to terminate the dribble and then pass fakes/shot fakes/pivots with the ball as defender pressures the ball and mirrors the ball with both hands. The sequence is shown in Figure A.

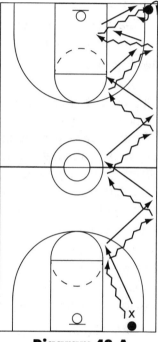

Diagram 48-A

Coaching Cues:

Maintain ball-you-basket position while pressuring ballhandler.
Live ball – active feet, prevent the drive, take away opponent's strength.
Dribble – get head on the ball, turn the dribbler, stop with your body.
Dead ball – stay in stance, attack ballhandler, mirror ball with both hands.

Coach:

Nolan Richardson, head coach at the University of Arkansas, holds the unique distinction of winning national championships at the junior college level and at NCAA I with the Arkansas Razorbacks. His teams are noted for playing aggressive pressure defense.

Horseshoe Drill
Summer of '80 Basketball Bulletin

Purpose:

Teach players how to defend the wing/forward player, both on and off the ball, in a man-to-man defense.

Description:

This drill starts with one offensive and one defensive player in the wing position, and one coach (player or manager) at each of the guard spots. Ball is on the strong side (Figure A).

Offensive player tries to get open to receive ball on wing while defensive player tries to deny the pass. If pass is made, they go one-on-one. If pass is not made, offensive player goes back door, defensive player still tries to deny pass (Figure B).

Offensive player then goes through to corner. Defensive player must then assume weakside defensive position, seeing both ball and man, and denying the flash pivot (Figure C). Ball is then passed from weakside to strongside and defense must close to wing denial position on this side of the court (Figure D).

Coaching Cues:

Deny the F lead, cover the back door, play one-on-one defense, assume weakside position, deny flash cuts to high post, deny the F lead.

Coach:

Don Kelbick was an assistant coach at Hofstra University during the 1980's.

Diagram 49-A   **Diagram 49-B**   **Diagram 49-C**   **Diagram 49-D**

Two-Man Contesting

Purpose:

Teach defenders to deny penetrating passes and defending 2-on-2 with coach as a feeder. Teaches both ballside and helpside defense.

Description:

Coach begins drill with ball in the middle of the floor (no helpside – both defenders are denying penetrating passes). As coach dribbles to one side, Figure A shows the ballside-helpside adjustment. X_2 forms a ball-you-man flat triangle, keeping vision on both 2 and 3. If 3 receives the ball, X_3 pressures the ball on ballside, with helpside defender X_2 moving to the middle of the FT lane.

If 3 drives, the helpside defender helps on penetration. If the drive is stopped, both defenders recover to their men (help and recover). When a shot is taken, they both block out.

Coaching Cues:

Defenders move as the ball moves, see the ball at all times, deny the entry pass, establish quick helpside on dribble or pass out of the middle of the floor (sprint to the ball), defend the drive (help and recover), and block out.

Diagram 50-A

Diagram 50-B

Coach:

Mike Krzyzcwski, known as "Coach K", played and coached at the United States Military Academy at West Point before establishing a legendary tradition at Duke University – 319 victories in 11 years, 90% graduation rate, eleven NCAA I bids, seven NCAA Final Fours, five ACC Championships, and two national championships.

DRILL
51

Defensive Post Drills
Fall '82 Basketball Bulletin

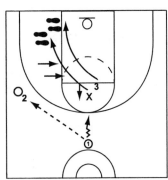

Diagram 51-A

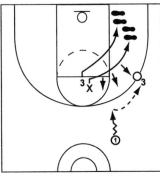

Diagram 51-B

Diagram 51-C

Purpose:

Teach defensive post players all skills needed to defend offensive post players.

Description:

Defensive post drills are developed and used in all entry situations.

Entry

A. Two side entry (Figure A)

B. Three side entry (Figure B)

C. Coaching points:

1. Establish defensive set at some point above the foul line. DO NOT SET UP DEEP IN THE LANE AND WAIT!

2. Force post to cut behind defender. DO NOT LET THE CUTTER "ACROSS YOUR FACE!"

3. Establish high front and deny the ball with ball side elbow in the lane.

4. Escort cutter to low post and establish low post front.

D. Nugget: In anticipation of pass from back to point and the postman stepping into the hole – DO NOT DROP LOW DEFENSIVE FOOT BELOW THE LEVEL OF THE POSTMAN'S TOP FOOT SO AS TO FACILITATE GETTING OVER THE TOP WHEN THE BALL IS RETURNED TO THE POINT.

E. Drill Progression: 2 and 3 men drive the baseline forcing defenders to a true low post front. 2 and 3 can shoot as both postmen work to boards. Defender "slips" inside if possible or over and opposite offensive man's turn.

Guard-to-Guard Line Adjustments (Figure C)

A. Coaching Points:

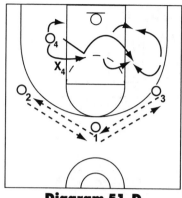

Diagram 51-D

1. Defender sets inside and above low post when ball is outside the area of the free throw line extended. He is one step off the line of the ball with vision in an "off the ball" defensive stance. He is thus in a position to deny a vertical cut to the ball or a corner release cut.

2. Defender moves with the pass opening up to the ball with a long first step as the post man cuts across the lane.

3. Step to position described in 1) above as post man sets up at completion of his cut.

4. Return ball to 1 man and repeat.

B. Nugget: Defender must move with each pass. Anticipate the pass!

C. Drill Progression: 3 cuts up the lane to ball and back down to low post. 3 releases to corner or wing and back to low post at beginning or end of drill.

Low Post Front (Figure D)

A. Coaching Points:

1. Defender starts in low post front – reacts to ball movement. Delay offense, then bring to ball.

2. Low post front is a 'V' front with elbow in the passing lane.

3. Defender must get "over" as ball is passed to – stop post man from stepping into hole.

4. As offense continues cut, defense makes every effort to get over all the way to low front as 3 receives the ball.

5. Also practice defender reacting to offense when he steps up into hole and then to opposite low post.

6. Repeat process as 3 passes to 4 and as 1 passes to 2.

B. Nugget: Defender can get from low front to top more effectively by "slipping" over. Lift back arm and step with back foot "slicing" over the post man.

C. Drill Progression: 4 cuts all the way to 2 and touches ball. Defender does the same. 4 then cuts to opposite low post as ball is passed to 3. Defender stays ball side and uses head snap if necessary.

Triangle Drill – High Post Denial (Figure E)

A. Coaching Points:

1. Defender sets two steps from post man and one step off the line of the ball for vision.

2. 4 cuts diagonally to a position half way into the top of the circle and outside the lane line. Defender escorts 4 man using short sliding adjustments and the elbow in the passing lane principle.

Diagram 51-E

Diagram 51-F

Diagram 51-G

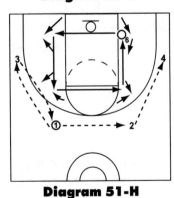

Diagram 51-H

3. As 3 passes to 1, defender gets over in a slip move stepping with back foot and lifting back arm. He then escorts 4 across lane staying ball side as ball is passed to 3.

4. 3 drives lane and 4 cuts to low post as defender escorts him down the lane and establishes low front.

B. Nugget: Stay over top if possible. As ball is passed from 1 to 3, defender may get caught behind 4. If so, beat him low and establish low front. Remember, defender can't get to cut-off mark if caught behind low post on ball side.

C. Drill Progression: Defender cuts off as 3 drives the baseline.

Guard to Forward – High Post (Figure F)

A. Coaching Points:

1. When 1 passes to 2 an adjustment is necessary. If the defender goes "over" the offense will get him on his back and take lead pass for layup.

2. The adjustment should be behind offensive center with a quick change in position to prevent post man from dropping low.

3. Establish position to block and hold as high as possible.

B. Nugget: Step with high foot then low foot as ball is passed.

C. Drill Progression: After defender establishes ball side set, 3 cuts away low and back to ball side low post. Defender does not follow 3 away but establishes line of the ball defense, escorts 3 across lane and establishes low post front. 2 can drive baseline and defender cuts off.

Medium Post Reaction (Figure G)

A. Coaching Points:

1. Establish inside post position with ball at 1. Ball is thrown back and forth with receiver holding for two seconds.

2. Defender gets over the top wherever possible. Go behind as last resort.

B. Nugget: Defender can't get to cut-off if caught behind.

The **NABC** Drill Book

C. Drill Progression: 2 drives and defender cuts off.

Four Corner – Multi-Purpose (Figure H)

A. Coaching Points:

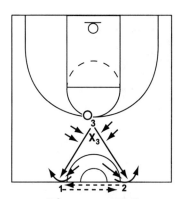

Diagram 51-I

1. Ball at 1 defender maintains defensive line as ball is passed to 3. 5 cuts to ball as defender escorts him through the lane and then establishes low front.

2. 3 returns ball to 1 and 5 cuts to high post. Defender maintains position with elbow in the lane.

3. 1 passes to 2 as 5 cuts across and defender goes over the top to high post.

4. 2 hits 4 as 5 goes down the lane with defender using snap around in getting to low front.

B. Nugget: Anticipate and move with every pass. Must take initiative in getting over the top.

C. Drill Progression: Call "lob" anytime ball is at 3 or 4 and defend with long step and jump.

High Post Release – Denial (Figure I)

A. Coaching Points:

1. 1 and 2 outside mid-court line and pass ball back and forth – defender adjusts his line.

2. Coach hollers "GO!" and 3 cuts to ball. Defender plays lead denial all the way to ball. Both 3 and defender touch ball.

B. Nugget: Defender must adjust his defensive split in accordance with distance between ball and his post.

C. Drill Progression: Defender must have the experience of stealing the ball and driving for layup.

Coaching Cues:

See Description section.

Coach:

Jerry Tarkanian, longtime UNLV coach where his team won an NCAA I championship, now coaches at Fresno State University (CA). His teams are noted for their aggressive pressure defense and up-tempo play.

4-on-4 Defend
Flex Drill

Diagram 52-A

Diagram 52-B

Diagram 52-C

Purpose:

Teach players in a drill breakdown situation to defend any designated offense or situation.

Description:

Place four defenders in a 4-on-4 shell defensive set. In order to drill against the "flex" offense, a pass from guard to corner is first made (Figure A). This is followed by a pass to the ball side guard spot and a guard to guard pass (Figure B). The drill continuity is shown in Figures C and D.

Coaching Cues:

A team needs to be able to defend basic offensive sets/ situations to be prepared for games. Coaches can design the 4-on-4 shell drill to practice defending most offensive situations. One of the most common is flex – defenders must pressure the ball, jump to the ball, fight through screens, defend one-on-one and communicate.

Coach:

University of North Dakota head coach Rich Glas has won over 350 games; nine years at UND and 24 years of coaching experience. He has also coached at Willamette University (OR) and University of Minnesota, Morris.

UCLA'S Defensive Cutthroat

Purpose:

Teach players 3-on-3, 4-on-4 defensive halfcourt skills under gamelike conditions.

Description:

♦ The only way to get points is to get stops on defense (play to certain number of points or for a period of time).

♦ If you take a charge, the game is over.

♦ Lines start at halfcourt (see Figure A).

♦ Offense scores then go to defense. New offense comes on court.

Coaching Cues:

♦ must close out in a stance.

♦ must stay in good stance – no statues!

♦ must talk – call picks, helpside, etc.

♦ every time ball is passed, you must jump to the ball.

♦ switch all picks, or no switch on picks, or switch cross picks only.

♦ trap all picks on ball or show and recover.

♦ box out – offensive rebounds result in defense going to end of line; offense then goes to defense.

♦ must front the post.

♦ fouls result in a basket – play D without fouling.

♦ take a charge and you win game regardless of score.

♦ must dive on loose balls.

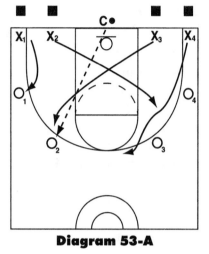

Diagram 53-A

Coach:

Steve Lavin, head coach of the fabled UCLA basketball program, where he succeeded Jim Harrick in 1996. He led his first team to the NCAA I tournament and is noted for his emphasis on fundamental skills and discipline.

4-on-4 Defensive Shell with Post and Corner Drive

Purpose:

Teach players team defensive skills of rotations on post passes and baseline drive penetrations.

Description:

Coach and four managers are aligned four offensive and defensive players, as shown in Figure A. The drill begins with coach passing to any offensive player. Offensive players may pass and catch on perimeter until the ball is passed to a corner (coach or manager). This person drives the baseline; opposite corner defender must stop drive, backside defender must rotate down (see Figure B) to take away baseline pass as "top" defenders sink to the level of the ball. On the pass back out they all scramble to pick up all offensive players and communicate their pickup.

Coaching Cues:

Check all defensive principles, stop baseline drive, rotate the backside, cover down on penetration (to level of ball), and talk - talk - talk.

Coach:

Kevin Eastman, Washington State University Couger head coach; spent three years at Belmont Abbey College, four years at University of North Carolina-Wilmington, and three years at WSU.

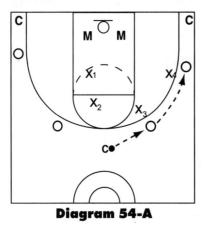

Diagram 54-A

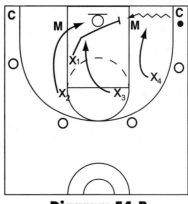

Diagram 54-B

4-Man Shell
with Situations

Purpose:

Teach team defense to cover and drill specific situations and skills:

- ♦ ballside/helpside
- ♦ jump to ball
- ♦ dribble penetration – help and switch or run and jump
- ♦ rotate on baseline drive.

Description:

4-on-4 halfcourt setup with different offensive situations emphasized each day. For example, deny penetrating passes, handling skip passes, guard penetration, forward penetration. Figures A, B show two situations.

Coaching Cues:

Pressure the ball, jump to the ball, helpside flat triangle (point your pistols), deny penetrating passes (hand in the lane).

Coach:

Lowell Roumph has become well known in community college circles whose teams play solid defense and disciplined offense. He started his coaching career in Nebraska (five years at Columbus St. Bonaventure) and has been at Northeastern (CO) CC for 30 years.

Diagram 55-A

Diagram 55-B

4-on-4 Defense
to Fast Break

Purpose:

Combine individual defensive drills into a team combination drill that also uses defense to offense transition.

Description:

This drill is run on alternate days, three times per week, when possible. It embodies all other half-court defensive skills and drills. Offensive players can flash to the post creating defensive post situations. The drill begins in the backcourt with defenders meeting opponents at the half-court line. A group of four stays on defense for a period of time, usually 5 minutes, as players rotate in on offense. Defenders fast break every time they get the ball – four new offensive players come in at that time.

Coaching Cue:

Communicate, be aggressive, deny passes, cover helpside defense, and block out on all shots. Play the ball tough and keep ball out of the post.

Coach:

Stan Morrison has led an illustrious career, from playing on California's 1959 NCAA I Championship team to now coaching at San Jose State University (7 years). He has coached at the University of Southern California (8 years), University of Pacific (7 years), and has been Conference/District Coach of the Year.

DRILL 57

Safety First Transition Drill

Purpose:

Teach offensive players to either rebound or go back to defense as a safety and then teach 2-on-1 defense.

Description:

Coach divides squad into groups of four; two on offense and two on defense. They begin drill playing 2-on-2 halfcourt (coach may restrict – ball screens, pass and cut, 2 dribble maximum, etc.). When shot is taken, offensive player closest to basket rebounds and teammate becomes safety by sprinting to half court. When defense gets the ball, they outlet it and create a 2-on-1 fast break against the safety. The offensive rebounder can either be taken out of the drill after the outlet or sprint to help the defender after the ball clears the top of the key.

Diagram 57-A

Coaching Cues:

After shot – always assume shot is missed (one player to safety, one rebound). Safety – sprint with vision, protect the basket (no layups), fake and force the extra pass to buy time for teammate to help.

Coach:

George Karl, head coach of the NBA Seattle Supersonics, has won championships with the CBA and Real Madrid Team in Spain. Karl was an All-American with Dean Smith at North Carolina in 1973.

DRILL 58

4-on-4 Recover

Purpose:

Teach players to get back on defense and help teammates who may be slow recovering. Offensive players drill on offensive fast break after rebounds.

Description:

The drill starts 4-on-4 halfcourt until a shot is taken (see Figure A). When the ball is rebounded by the defensive team (you can take it out and fast break on made baskets also), they outlet the ball on the fast break. The offensive team sprints to defense with the exception of the shooter who must touch the baseline before going to defense. The situation is 4-on-3 until player who shot recovers to defense, then regular defense is carried out.

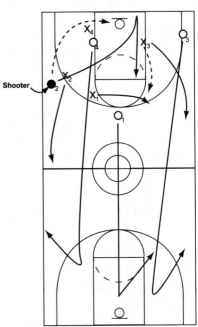

Coaching Cues:

Defense – sprint to halfcourt, catch your man if he is ahead or turn around and find your man if he is behind you. Get in a stance on the halfcourt, closest man takes the ball, rest picking up an opponent. Play the full possession on D until you steal or rebound the ball. Offense – top speed under control, find the open man.

Diagram 58-A

Coach:

Coach Wimp Sanderson, University of Arkansas-Little Rock, has won 636 games and lost 375 as a head and assistant coach. He is in his 4th year at UALR, after 12 head coaching years at Alabama and a 20-year stint as assistant there. Sanderson is well known as a great communicator with players.

Ohio U.
No Hands/Hell

Purpose:

Improve team defensive fundamentals, techniques, and positioning. Improve communication, concentration and toughness, and emphasize the concept that a team is only as good as its weakest link.

Description:

This is a 5-on-5 team defense drill that starts on the quarter-court (top of key). Defenders must play defense with hands behind their backs. After 30 seconds, the defense can use their hands and must not allow the offense to score for the full duration of the possession (using the shot clock).

After a turnover or rebound, the defensive team makes a D to O transition (5-on-0) to a score. The original offensive team remains at their basket preparing to play offense again. After the 5-on-0 transition basket is made, the team sprints back to defense again (no hands for first 30 seconds). The coach is at halfcourt and can pass to an offensive player at any time.

Repeat this sequence 3-5 consecutive times. If the offense makes a layup in the first 30 seconds or scores at any time, the defense must start over again until they meet the consecutive stops on defense goal.

Coaching Cues:

Defenders follow all basic principles – pressure ball, deny leads, ball-you-man help position, jump to the ball, front the post, fight through screens, and block out. Find a way to make it happen.

Coach:

Larry Hunter, head coach of Ohio University, has an overall record of 447-169 (.726) in 21 seasons of coaching. At Wittenberg, his team won the NCAA III title his first year (1977), with four other Final Four appearances. His teams are noted for their fundamentals.

UCONN
12-Man Shell

Purpose:

Teach players team skills of half-court and full-court defense.

Description:

Divide your top twelve players into three teams of four. Each team rotates in to play defense. The coach begins the drill with the ball at the top of the key. He passes to any offensive player and the defenders must react to reach correct position. Allow the offense 3-4 passes to move ball and players, without the defense being allowed to touch the ball (be in correct stance and position). We then blow a whistle to signal the defense to try to score.

Each day we have a different emphasis – such as preventing penetration (that day offensive players would dribble drive every time they catch the ball).

Points are given for each defensive possession (0-5 points) and keep score for 10-20 minutes per day. Keep

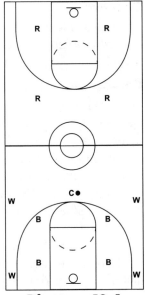

Diagram 60-A

the same teams for 4-5 days and then let the seniors pick different teams.

The transition element (O-to-D) can be added by having the third team wait to play defense at the opposite end of the court (see Figure A). The Red team (R) is waiting to play defense against the Blue team (B), who is defending against the White team (W).

Coaching Cues:

Pressure the ball, talk, deny leads, closeout under control, jump to the ball, rotate on penetration, take a charge, contest the shot, bump cutters, trap the screen and roll, help and recover, and box out on every shot.

Coach:

In 11 seasons at Connecticut, Jim Calhoun's teams have compiled an overall record of 240-114. During the past 10 seasons, UCONN teams have averaged over 23 wins per season, the winningest period in their 97 year history. In addition, UCONN is now a regular participant in postseason play and annually ranks in the Top 20 teams in the country.

DRILL
61

4-on-4
Half-court Games

Purpose:

Teach players to prevent defensive breakdowns (defend before your man gets the ball). Also teaches offensive players good shot selection.

Description:

In a half-court format, play 15 minutes of 4-on-4 games. Games are to 4 baskets with "winners out." Coach lets play get physical, but clean; only make positive comments, little teaching, a true competitive game situation. When your team scores, you retain ball (make it, take it). Clear ball to top of key on each possession. All other players underneath basket with coach. They encourage good plays. When one team reaches 4 baskets, the new team comes in on offense.

Coaching Cues:

See who wins and why – usually shot selection/patience on offense or breakdowns defensively.

Coach:

Warren Friedrichs has 22 years head coaching experience and ten Coach-of-the-Year awards, including 1996 NAIA Div. II National Coach of the Year. He has spent the last 13 years at Whitworth College in Spokane, WA where his teams have won four Northwest Conference titles and have gone to two NAIA II national tournaments (2nd in 1996).

DRILL 62

UTEP's
Defensive Drills
Winter '78 Basketball Bulletin

Purpose:

Teach players the specific defensive skills needed in the UTEP man-to-man defense.

Description:

There are three basic principles that are necessary to have a good defensive team. They are: 1) control the tempo; 2) basket protection; and 3) shot selection with good execution and patience. In controlling the tempo, it is quite necessary that your team is very capable, as far as the transition game is concerned. The dribbler must be stopped at the 10-second line, and five people must get in front of the ball as quickly as possible. This is why during practices, they do not use halfcourt situations. Their drills are full court most of the time.

As far as basket protection is concerned, we divide the front-court into three areas (see Figure A). No shots should be given up in section A, and the shooting percentage goes down when you make your opponent shoot from sections B and C. UTEP uses their shooting charts not just to tell what kind of shooting percentage they or their opponents have, but to see how many shots are taken in each of the prescribed areas.

As far as shot selection is concerned, we describe a good shot for each player. The things that are necessary in this description are the game situations. By that, we mean score, time of game, and which of your players is taking the shot. Execution of offense and patience are very important concepts, as far as your total defense is concerned. We will use slow down, or delay type game for offensive possessions, especially when they are playing on the road, or when their overall talent is less than their opponents. By using this particular offensive strategy, it will make his defense better, and also will keep the score closer for possible road victory.

Individual Defense Rules. UTEP players do not use a square stance, they use a stride stance. They have their hands in a position so they can move as quickly as possible. We do not do slide drills. It is our philosophy that as soon as the player moves, they go to a run, rather than a slide, because we want players to get from one position to another as quickly

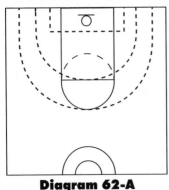

Diagram 62-A

as possible, and you do that by running. As far as closeness to the offensive player is concerned, we try to put their head and shoulders into the offensive player, and watch his waist, not the ball. Another rule that is definitely stressed is that you do **not** fight the ball when it is being dribbled. When it comes to post defense, we do not wish to have their players lay on the post. We want to stay at least three feet away, and closer to the ball than the person they are defending. When they are playing on the offside defense, it is important that we stay below the line between the person we are defending and the ball. When we have our head pointed straight ahead, we can see both the man and the ball at the same time. But if you lose sight of one of them, it is imperative that you lose sight of your man, and not the ball. When defending cutters, it is our feeling that you always stay to the ball side of your man. During most of our drills, they will not switch.

Drills. The progression of the drills are as follows:

1. Spot Drill. In this situation, all four players remain stationary, and what is trying to be developed, is each player moves as the ball is moved; each player protects the middle, tries to instill the importance of the offside man away from the ball. Don't slide, but run when the ball is moved (Figure B).

   Rules:
   - Offense must be stationary
   - Every defender moves on each pass
   - Don't slide – run on each defensive move
   - Don't deny leads
   - Sink away from the ball
   - See man and ball at same time
   - Protect the baseline

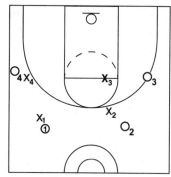

Diagram 62-B

2. Pick and Help Drill. No switch. Go over the top most of the time, but can go behind. Defensive man off the ball must hold up the dribble (Figure C).

   Rules:
   - No switch
   - X_1 can go over on behind screen
   - X_2 holds up dribble until X_1 can get there

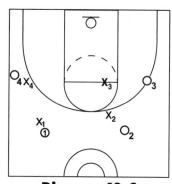

Diagram 62-C

3. Guard and Cutter Drill (4-on-4). (Figure D) Drill is for offside help and defending the cutter.

   Rules:
   - 2 passes to 3, X_2 must be on ballside of 2
   - X_1, X_2, X_4 must move to ball

Diagram 62-D

4. 3-on-3 – Defense Drill. (Figure E). Options used are: Reaction, Weave, Pass and Pick, Pass and Pick Away, and Pass and Cut

Rules:

- ◆ Reaction – defense reacts to dribbler, man on ball
- ◆ Weave – no switch, X_1 goes behind on ball exchange, X_2 and X_3 stay up
- ◆ Pass and Pick – no switch, X_1 does not follow screener, stays in help position for X_2 and X_3
- ◆ Pass and Pick Away – X_1 stays in middle and helps X_2 or X_3 avoid screen
- ◆ Pass and Cut – X_1 must get on ball side as 1 passes to 2, 3 comes to ball.

Diagram 62-E

Coaching Cues:

Emphasis is placed on UTEP defensive principles – stride stance, quick hands, run (not slide) movement, watch the waist of ballhandler, don't fight the dribbler, see the ball at all times, and defend cutters on the ballside.

Coach:

Coach Don "Bear" Haskins has been coaching at UTEP since 1961; 14 NCAA I berths and seven NIT trips, and over 700 wins. In 1966, his all-black Texas Western team won the NCAA I championship. Coach Haskins was inducted into the Basketball Hall of Fame in 1997.

Pride Drill

Purpose:

Teach players offensive to defensive team transition.

Description:

Start 5-on-0 going from defense to offense – fill offensive lanes and score from primary or secondary fast break. Players keep tipping ball until coach blows whistle, then all players sprint to defense and find a mythical opponent at the opposite end of the court. Defenders "chop feet" until coach blows whistle and new team comes on the floor to repeat sequence. Coach gives 0-3 points for execution and hustle. Drill is completed when entire squad reaches a prescribed point goal, e.g., 15, 21. See Figure A.

Creates great enthusiasm, conditioning and team defensive pride. End every practice with this drill.

Coaching Cues:

Sprint to defense as you see the ball. Safety has basket responsibility and other four defenders sprint to "point" (FT lane), find ball and play defense with active feet until the whistle blows.

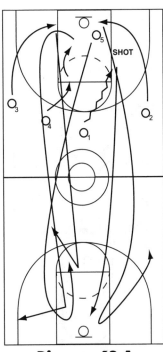

Diagram 63-A

Coach:

Dan Miles has been head man at Oregon Tech for 26 years (541-274), had eleven "Top 20" NAIA teams, and has been inducted into the Oregon Sports Hall of Fame.

Basic 6 Drills to Better Defense

Spring '86 Basketball Bulletin

Purpose:

Teach players all basic man-to-man defensive skills with six daily drills.

Diagram 64-A

Diagram 64-B

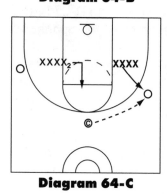

Diagram 64-C

Description:

Defense has been the cornerstone of our success as we operate under the practice theory of the late Maury John (former Drake University coach) the "Defense Daily Develops Defense."

We feel that more practice time should be given to offense since timing and proper execution are so vital to offensive success. Offense entertains, but defense wins. With this in mind, we have developed six basic defensive drills which we do almost daily. These drills are done with intensity and total concentration, but they do not consume a lot of practice time.

Driving Line (Figure A)

The defense must force the ball sideline, contain the dribbler, cut off the baseline and pressure the dribbler when he picks up the dribble. We do not allow the offense to shoot. This is our basic drill for containing the man with the ball. (Both sides work at the same time).

Close Out 1-1 (Figure B)

Alternate each side. Defense pitches ball to offense and closes out hard with baseline foot back (inside foot up) and front hand up to bother shooter. Defense must cut off baseline on low drive or force ball out of key on high drive. The key points of the drill are to force a perimeter shot over pressure and do not get beat on the first dribble. Players rotate from defense to offense. Block out the shooter.

Close Out 2-2 (Figure C)

Coach will pass ball to a wing. Defense must immediately react to ball side close out and help side posi-

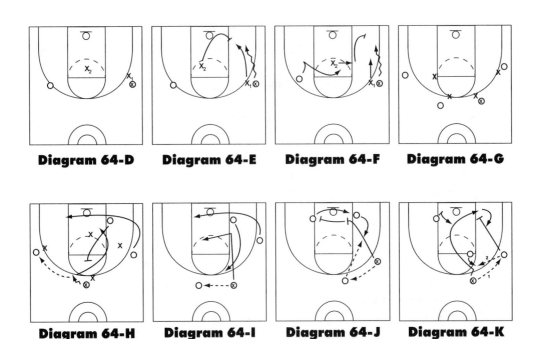

Diagram 64-D   **Diagram 64-E**   **Diagram 64-F**   **Diagram 64-G**

Diagram 64-H   **Diagram 64-I**   **Diagram 64-J**   **Diagram 64-K**

tion. As shown in Figure D, X_1 must pressure – contain the ball while X_2 gets to help position in **middle** of key pointing at ball and man. The offense plays 2-on-2 trying to score. In Figure E, if offense drives, X_2 must release and immediately help X_1 cut off drive by offense. On pass from driver to receiver, defense must quickly recover. We teach X_2 to help as soon as offense starts a drive. We want to over-help! In Figure F, X_2 must cut off any flash cutter and still help X_1. Again, players rotate from defense to offense. This is a tough drill, but it is vital to good defense – man or zone.

4-4 Combo (Figure G)

This is the basic shell drill that almost everyone uses. We do not allow the offense to shoot. The defense stays for 30-40 seconds and we switch offense to defense. We do not contest passes above the free throw line and we make our help side defender get to the middle of the court in line with the basket. We deny all penetrating passes (wing, flash cutter, post) and we close out hard on all perimeter players. Our defense forces sideline so we try to keep ball out of the middle. In order to make the 4-4 combo effective (see Figure H), we vary the drill to conform with different offenses we will face during the season. This diagram shows a one-guard front with possible backscreens. See Figure I for flex set with backscreen and screen-down opportunities, and Figure J – passing game screen-down and screen-across opportunities. Figure K depicts a UCLA high post set.

There are endless other offensive schemes that can be incorporated into the 4-4 combo. The offense executes with game intensity and the defense reacts. No shots. Five to eight minutes of intense drill work in the 4-4 combo is needed daily. Vary your sets daily.

Diagram 64-L

3-3 Half Court (Figure L)

This drill is used to work on ball screens. Offense must start with screen situation and then play 3-on-3. Talk is crucial. We "switch," "stay" or "slide through" on the command! Rotate offense to defense. The 4-4 combo and the 3-3 half court are used as part of the pre-game warm-up routine.

3-3 Full Court (Figure M)

This is a hard drill. Players must "gut up" to be successful. Offense cannot throw long pass. Defense must pressure man-to-man and contain ball. Help man will cut off middle of floor. Force ball to sideline. When O shoots, they go to defense coming back and X is on offense. After one trip up and back full court, original defense will stay on floor and new offense will come on. We make original defense stay for 4 or 5 full trips. This is very demanding, but we usually have great spirit and intensity during the drill.

Figure N depicts a variation of 3-3 full court – a quick double team on the ball and retreat when offense passes it out. Again, no long passes allowed.

These basic 6 drills teach our defensive concepts whether we ar playing man or zone defense. Whatever our defense is at a particular time we try to do several key things:

1. Pressure – contain basketball.
2. Close down the middle.
3. Close out hard on all passes.
4. Play with intensity.

When we play zone it is still with our principles learned from these basic 6 drills. We use the whole method of 5 defense versus 7 offense to get our proper zone slides. These drills take up 30-35 minutes of practice time and help to lay a solid defensive foundation, regardless of whether we play man or zone defense during the game.

Coaching Cues:

This 30-minute drill package focuses on the concept that "defense daily develops defense." This concept was popularized by Maury John of Drake University, whose teams were well known for solid pressure defense.

Coach:

Frank Evans wrote this article when he was head coach at Kaskaskia Community College (IL) during the 1980s.

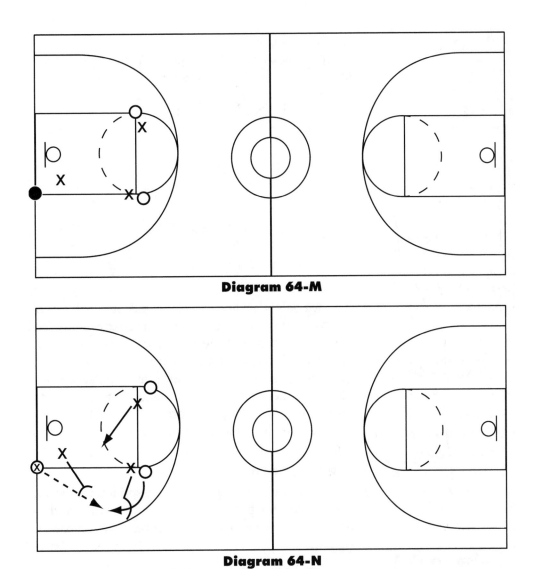

Diagram 64-M

Diagram 64-N

5-on-4 plus 1
Transition Drill

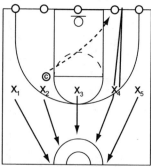

Diagram 65-A

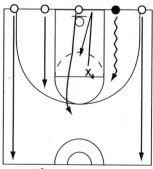

Diagram 65-B

Purpose:

Teach players to cover the basket (prevent easy scores), stop the ball, pick up open men and communicate when making the transition from offense to defense.

Description:

Five defenders line up on the halfcourt with five offensive players on the baseline. The coach has the ball and passes to one of the offensive players, as seen in Figure A. The player guarding the ballhandler must touch the baseline before transitioning to defense – all other defenders transition immediately as offensive players bearing the ball up the floor on the fast break (Figure B). The defensive team must execute an effective transition to defense, as seen in Figure C.

Coaching Cues:

When transitioning to defense, sprint back with vision, protect the basket first, then find shooters and get a man (not necessarily yours) as you <u>communicate</u>.

Coach:

Tom Asbury heads the Kansas State Wildcat program (4th year) after six successful years at Pepperdine University. He has led his teams into postseason play six times.

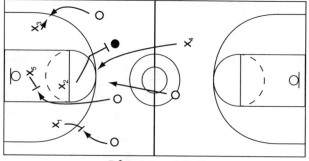

Diagram 65-C

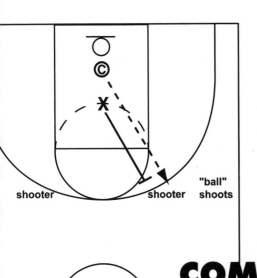

shooter   shooter   "ball" shoots

COMBINATION
DRILLS

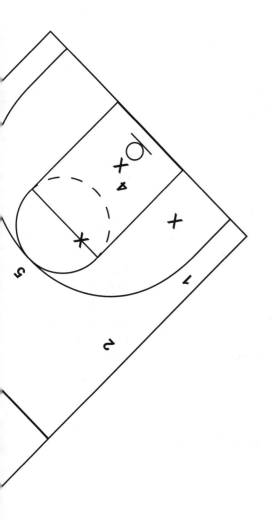

Mimetics Drills

Purpose:

Teach players fundamental skills by having the coach demonstrate the skill with players mimicking the movements.

Description:

As an ideal class program the mimetics of basketball furnish all the motivation necessary for teaching basic fundamentals around which all types of plays evolve.

For example, a group of children in the gymnasium classes could be more easily led to strive for better stances in both offensive and defensive positions if they were told and shown that John Doe, the high-school star athlete, executed his fundamentals thus.

In this type of motivation, no one should handle the ball except the instructor who demonstrates the play. One of the class members should work with him in the demonstration. In order to hold a large class in floor formation it will be necessary to alter follow-throughs somewhat, but the nature of the alteration should serve to increase the value of the exercises <u>as a basketball drill</u>. All exercises can be performed on the individual floor assignment. Changing the class positions is thus avoided.

The exercises should be performed and the follow-through made with an avoidance of tensing the muscles. The smooth and seemingly effortless basketball player is the imaginative model to follow. As a cat stretches itself to health, so should the versatile basketball player of the future unlimber his shooting muscles.

A class of 40 to 50 can be handled in this manner without difficulty. All members of the class should execute the same fundamentals until every type of play on both offense and defense has been fairly well mastered. Every coach will differ somewhat in methods of teaching, and no two coaches will stress the same fundamentals.

It is the author's hope herein to sell to the coaches the idea of <u>teaching shadow basketball</u> to immature youngsters before permitting them to handle the ball. By watching the coach-instructor demonstrate the play with the ball and then by being directed to go slowly through the mechanics of the play without the ball, junior-high-school boys will acquire the correct mechanics of fundamental basketball before they reach high school.

Editor's Note: This section on effective use of drills to teach fundamental skills was developed by the <u>first</u> basketball coach, Phog Allen.

After the more simple fundamentals have been mastered the groups can then work in pairs. Alternate rows can handle the imaginary ball, while the other rows can act as guards and face them, constantly keeping their 3-ft. distance from the ballhandlers by the use of guard steps.

Coaches can teach shooting, faking, dribbling, stops and pivots, defense and other movement fundamentals with this mass drill.

Coaching Cues:

Focus on the fundamentals.

Coach:

This drill information was taken from the book *Better Basketball* by Forrest "Phog" Allen, the first basketball coach (at Baker University and later at the University of Kansas). Allen was an early inductee into the Basketball Hall of Fame.

Daily Practice Fundamental Drills

Spring '86 Basketball Bulletin

Purpose:

Teach players the movement of balance and quickness in basic stance and steps drills, as well as in a fast break drill.

Description:

I have always been very interested in basketball and I don't think I will ever lose my interest as long as I am around. I have probably spoken at more clinics than anyone. I have attended more than almost anyone, because I started attending as a high school player with my coach.

Two things I wanted in players:

1. Balance
2. Quickness under control.

These were my ideas as a high school coach and my thoughts never changed once I went to college, and it would not change today even if I were coaching the professionals. I wanted quickness. Did I want size? Yes of course I did, but where some of my peers wanted size, I would sacrifice some size for speed and quickness. I believe that the most important thing in basketball, just as in life, is balance. Physical, mental, and emotional balance. Physical balance, how do we get it? I started every practice every day with drills for physical balance. We started out with feet as wide as the shoulders, head mid-point above the feet, chin up so you can see and vision is not impaired. Hands in front and close to the body. Joints flexed and relaxed, trying for this at all times offensively and defensively.

Everyone on the floor at 3:15 PM. No exceptions! We started on time and ended on time. Our players knew when we were starting and when it ended. We tried to do a good job of preparing our players for games and performance of games depends on how good you practice. At 3:29 1 blew my whistle and my players knew immediately where to go.

Diagram 67-A

Basic position for drills – 3 lines spread on the halfcourt facing midcourt. All drills done without a ball (see Diagram A).

1. Two minutes in position to loosen up on your own. Stretch, bend, turn, squat, twist. Move every joint, head, shoulders, muscles; I am talking to them all the time.

2. Position for jump shot. Checking form, I am looking for balanced position.

3. Shot. Looking for proper form without the ball.

4. Freeze the defense and shoot. Freeze defense with body and head fakes. (No ball fakes).

5. Go by the defense. Raise defensive man by fake and go by him and not around.

6. Position for jump ball. Hands shoulder height. Explode with jump.

7. Offensive rebounding. The most important things about rebounding are:

   A. Assume the shot will be missed.

   B. Hands above your shoulders with palms forward.

   C. Go get the ball. Go by defense right and left.

   D. You missed it. Go right up and tip it.

   E. You can do the same thing without tipping the ball; use the two-hand rip.

   F. Go up, get the ball with two hands, bring the ball close to your chest, make one pump and go back up strong.

8. Defensive rebounding.

   A. Assume shot will be missed.

   B. Hands above your shoulders, with palms forward.

   C. Use cross-over step or reverse pivot to get in path of offensive man. Do not blockout, go hard for good strong rebound.

   D. Get the ball and bring it to the chest, turn and make the outlet pass.

These drills were used every day. Work on technique and balance. Balance in my opinion is the most important thing in playing the game of basketball and living our normal life. You must keep things in perspective. Think of the balance you must have in playing the game – physical balance, team balance, rebounding balance, court balance and squad balance. Then we would put players on the baseline.

Diagram 67-B

Baseline Drills (Diagram B)

1. Change of direction.

2. Change of pace to mid-court, defensive sliding back to line.

3. Repeat drills in pairs and reverse at mid-court.

4. 1-on-1 dribbling and defense with ball. No behind-the-back or through-the-legs dribbling. All rules apply to all and stick with it.

All drills are conditioning drills and all are basketball drills. Always working on balance. I don't believe in running for conditioning. I don't believe in running stairs. I don't believe in running cross country. I believe in short sprints, often repeated.

Now I am going to show you what I think was the best drill I had. I like to use this drill for ten minutes a practice. Hardly a day went by, except the day before a game, that we didn't use this drill. Now in my book I called this a conditioning drill; I shouldn't have called it that, because I didn't want them to think this was some kind of punishment. You can use this drill with any number of players, depending on the number you have on the squad. We are getting a lot of things from this drill: 3-on-2 defensively and offensively, and we are getting conditioning. The following is the way we start the drill:

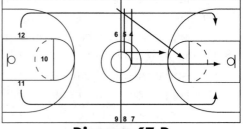

Diagram 67-C

3-on-2 Full Court Continuity
(see Diagram C)

Defense starts at top of circle and medium post. Number 2 puts ball on board, gets rebound and starts down the floor either on dribble or may make one pass to side, but we want the ball back in to middle man by mid-court. When ball is halfway between two circles, trailer defensive man #10 may enter into defense, offense should only have enough time for one or two passes before the shot.

Diagram 67-D

Reverse or Continuity
(see Diagram D)

On turnover, made or missed basket defense #10, 11 and 12 rebounds and move to opposite end. As shot was taken #4 and 5 move to center circle and retreat to defense. Number 10, 11 and 12 will bring ball back against #4 and 5. Number 6 will be trailer defense. After #10, 11 and 12 start down the floor #1, 2 and 3 will return to their respective lines. The continuity continues up and down the court for as long as you like. We do this for the first week.

2nd Week: We tell last offensive man to touch the ball to play defense to mid-court.

3rd Week: We have all three offensive men to play defense back to mid-court. This makes a good drill for offensive to defensive transition.

Coaching Cues:

All coaching cues are identified in Description – the coaching focus is on the concepts of balance and quickness.

Coach:

John Wooden, inducted in the Basketball Hall of Fame as a player and coach, is considered by many as the greatest coach in the history of the game. He has always focused on fundamental skills.

DRILL 68

Diagram-8
Rebounding

Purpose:

Teach players ball control while tipping and rebounding as a conditioning drill.

Description:

Three players and a ball at each basket as shown in Diagram A, with ball starting on overload side. Player 3 tosses ball on an angle above basket and across backboard to create a rebound for player 4. As this is done the rebounder always moves behind and to the opposite side (tip/rebound and go behind), as shown in Diagram B. Player 4 rebounds the ball and tips/tosses it back on the backboard to player 2, then goes behind 2 for the next exchange.

Diagram 68-A

Diagram 68-B

Younger players may leap to catch the ball with two hands, come down and chin the ball, then jump up to shoot the ball on the backboard to the opposite side. Older players may tip the ball back and forth with two-hand tips. A coach may designate a given number of consecutive tips/rebounds (e.g., 15, 20, 25) to complete or go for a designated time (e.g., 1, 2, 3 minutes). The last player always finishes with a made basket.

Coaching Cues:

Use two-hand two-feet rebound technique. Tipping – keep ball high, fully extend arms, tip with wrists and fingertips. Rebounding – reach up with two hands to capture ball at peak of jump, chin the ball with elbows out and fingertips up. Go back up to toss/shoot ball high on the backboard. Emphasize balance and control.

Coach:

The editor, Jerry Krause, adapted this drill from Coach John Wooden, the legendary UCLA coach who first made it famous. Coach Wooden used it regularly in his practices.

Bronx
Rebounding Drill

Purpose:

Teach players aggressive rebounding style and scoring in traffic.

Description:

Three players at a time are in the free throw lane. Coach has ball at the free throw line, as seen in Diagram A. Coach shoots and all players attempt to capture the rebound with two hands. A player must score two baskets before being replaced by another player from out-of-bounds.

Coaching Cues:

No dribbling is allowed. Keep ball up with two hands on ball at all times. Score two baskets and you are out.

Coach:

Matt Kilcullen is head coach at Western Kentucky, where he is entering his 20th year of college coaching. Matt was Sun Belt Conference Coach of the Year in 1994 (Jacksonville) and 1995 (WKU).

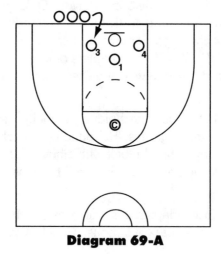

Diagram 69-A

4-on-3 Passing Drill

Purpose:

Teach offensive players to improve passing/catching skills and move without the ball. Teach defensive players to defend when there is a mismatch (outnumbered) with the offense.

Description:

Four offensive players start the ball at midcourt (Diagram A). As seen in Diagram A, the three defensive players form a triangle with one player at the FT line and the other two on each block. The four offensive players pass and cut (as shown in Diagram A) to the positions seen in Diagram B; a two guard front with two wings. One guard passes to the other guard and cuts through the lane with the wing on the passer's side rotating up (Diagram B). Diagram C illustrates a guard–wing pass, cut to basket and replace.

Offense wants to keep the ball moving with as little dribbling as possible. Offense passes and cuts hard to the basket, looking for an easy basket. No screening involved. Simple passing and cutting. Drill helps the offense learn to move without the ball with sharp, purposeful cuts. (Diagram D) Defense learns to play against numerical disadvantages. All cutters should receive a body check from the defense. Hands should be up, moving; constantly trying to get a deflection. All three players should be talking, communicating about cutter. Coaches should encourage defensive players to get physical, aggressive.

At end of each possession, four more offensive players should step up and start the drill again for

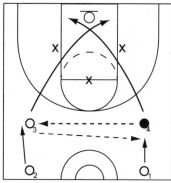

Diagram 70-A

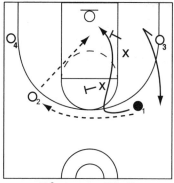

Diagram 70-B

Diagram 70-C

mid-court.

Coaching Cues:

Diagram 70-D

Offense: Always make crisp passes. Each cut is a sharp one with the cutter holding his hands up "asking for the ball." Cuts should always be set up with misdirection. Off the ball, replace the cutter quickly. Be aggressive and attack the basket. Offense has a rebounding advantage because of 4 on 3 numerical advantage.

Defense: Always body check offensive cutters. Have your hands up and moving in the passing lanes. Communicate on each offensive cut. Protect the basket, no shots in the paint. Give up a jump shot from outside rather than a layup. No uncontested shots. Try for a deflection on every pass. Block out and rebound!

Coach:

Georgia State's head coach, Charles "Lefty" Driesell is one of college basketball's all-time winningest coaches with close to 700 game victories. Driesell remains the winningest head coach in Davidson, Maryland, and James Madison basketball history. Eight times Driesell has been honored as a conference coach of the year, and 17 times his teams have captured either regular season or conference tournament titles.

3-on-3 Full-Court – No Dribble Drill

Purpose:

Teach players to create a lead, use proper footwork while passing and catching against full court pressure defense.

Description:

The full court is divided into three lanes with an offensive player and defensive player in each lane where the offensive team must advance the ball from baseline to baseline. This is illustrated in Diagram A.

3-on-3 Full-Court No Dribble (Diagram B)

Ball starts in the middle. Middle man can throw it to either wing trying to create a lead. The ball cannot be skipped from wing to wing; it must go thru the middle man, then it may go to either wing.

Rules:

1. NO dribbles.
2. NO lobs; you must come back to get the ball.
3. You must get the ball from one baseline to the other.
4. Players must stay in their lanes.

Coaching Cues:

Create a lead (passing lane) using quick v-cuts and backdoor moves to get open up the floor, but coming back to the ball. Catch and face when receiving the ball – receivers should get close to defenders to get open.

Coach:

Dick Davey is head coach of Santa Clara University. He has a long and distinguished career as a high school coach (5 years at Leland High School, San Jose, CA), assistant at University of California (5 years), assistant at Santa Clara (15 years).

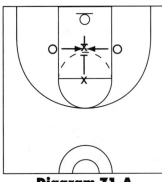

Diagram 71-A

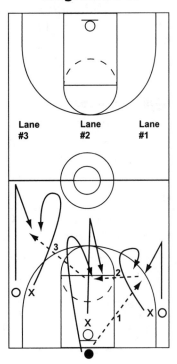

Diagram 71-B

Stops - Starts - Turns - Live Double Down

DRILL 72

Purpose:

Teach offensive players to dribble drive, jump stop, pivot and face (swoop ball), post up and receive pass, pass to post, and cut off post. Teach defensive players to closeout on ball, defend wing player, double down on post player, and recover to assigned offensive player.

Description:

Three players to a basket, as shown in the diagram (O_1, X_2, O_3). O_1 dribble drives to the operational area on wing as X_2 closes out with inside foot up to prevent the drive to the middle of the court. O_1 swoops ball to face basket as O_3 posts up on block. O_1 passes to post as X_2 contests pass (inside hand up to contest skip pass, outside hand contests post pass). O_3 shows numbers to ball, catches pass with both hands, and chins ball. X_2 closes down on high side of post O_3 as O_1 cuts to elbow for possible pass from post. O_3 fakes pass to O_1 and dribble drives to wing operational area, O_1 becomes defender and closes out on O_3, as original X_2 becomes the post player. The whole sequence is repeated – may switch sides.

Coaching Cues:

Coaches emphasis on specific techniques used in your system – dribble drive, stops, turns, pass to post, catch, defend closeout, post pass and double down (1-on-1 offense and defense). Passer becomes closeout defender, defender becomes post player, and post player becomes passer.

Coach:

George Pfeiffer, Head Coach, Lewis-Clark State College (Idaho), 9 years at L-C and a 20-year coaching career, with two championships.

Diagram 72-A

Diagram 72-B

Diagram 72-C

Emphasizing the Basics

Winter '86 Basketball Bulletin

Purpose:

Develop drills that emphasize basic concepts of your basketball program.

Description:

Coaches at all levels of organized basketball have often advocated the "KISS" (Keep It Simple, Stupid!) philosophy when coaching their teams. Basketball can be a relatively simple game if players properly execute the basic fundamentals. Successful coaches have long stressed the importance of simplicity, and warned of the dangers of deploying strategies and tactics too difficult, too complex, or too numerous for the talents and abilities of their players.

At times, however, it is difficult to resist the temptation to look for shortcuts or gimmicks to gain a competitive edge. Or, there is the desire to emulate the game plans and techniques of highly successful high school, college, or professional teams. In most cases, shortcuts are either short-lived or seldom applicable to all situations. Also, careful consideration must be given to the physical and mental capabilities of your own team and of your own teaching abilities when trying to duplicate the styles of play of other teams.

What has proven to be true is that the teams that are effective in executing the basic fundamentals of the game rarely have "off nights" or "beat" themselves. With the thought of simplicity in mind while emphasizing the basics, the "Raider Rules" were developed. This list of rules is nothing new, but is an attempt to be simple yet complete enough to cover most game situations.

If our team can consistently execute each one of these basic fundamentals, we believe we will be an extremely difficult team to beat. The key, of course, is to get our players to perform these basics in all game and practice situations. Therefore, our players are not only drilled repetitively, they are also expected to be able to recognize and verbalize proper execution of fundamentals.

Raider Rules

1. <u>Move without the Ball</u>: The easiest player to defend is one who stands still on offense. Movement with a definite purpose is better, but even "no-purpose" movement is probably better than standing still. Any movement that causes the defensive man to adjust, or forces him to split his attention from the ball, is productive for the offense.

2. <u>Handle the Ball</u>: The emphasis here is on making the easy or percentage play as opposed to the difficult or spectacular play. A study of our team and our

opponents showed more turnovers resulting from the offense's "unforced errors" than the defensive team's pressure. Many of these ballhandling mistakes were made when players tried to make too good of a play, or plays they lacked the skill or talent to execute. Most coaches would rather have "great players" than "great plays." Great players make the good play nearly every time.

3. Shoot Good Shots: This sounds simple but is often a very difficult fundamental to teach. Players need to learn what is meant by a "good" shot. We believe good shots are determined by three factors: 1) the shooting range of the shooter (it varies from player to player and the more objectively it can be determined, the better); 2) the amount of defensive pressure on the shooter; and 3) the game situation.

Again, these are simple concepts that can be applied to almost every situation. How a coach goes about teaching ball pressure, post denial, shot selection, etc., is going to be determined by his own basketball philosophy. There are other fundamentals that obviously will be taught and each coach will emphasize the things he feels are most important for his team.

This list of "Raider Rules" is posted in the locker room and is given to the players for their notebooks. Players are evaluated on their execution of these fundamentals more than anything else. Our goal is to not only get each player to recognize proper execution of these basics in his own play, but to recognize it also in the play of his teammates and opponents.

The following are some of our favorite drills for emphasizing the basics in the "Raider Rules."

Talk on Defense

"Talk" can be emphasized in any defensive drill. However, we have found that in drills involving several players (4-on-4, 5-on-5, etc) it is more difficult to concentrate on which players are, and which players are not, communicating effectively. The drills using two or three defensive players are best since each player is usually involved in the action. Of course you can also emphasize other defensive funda-

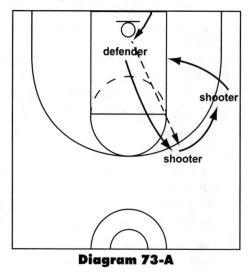

Diagram 73-A

mentals in these drills, but the key to improving defensive "talk" is for the players to understand that their communications are the focal point of the drills.

Defensive Pressure and Ball Containment

The best drill we have found to emphasize this rule is 1-on-1 defense on the ball after approaching the ball from a weakside help position (Diagram A).

The coach (C) starts with the ball and makes sure X_1 is in the proper weakside help position. C throws the crosscourt lob pass to 0_1. X_1 must approach under control to contain 0_1's drive, but must also

Diagram 73-B

Diagram 73-C

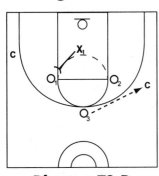

Diagram 73-D

Diagram 73-E

be close enough to pressure the jump shot of O_1. To determine if X_1 has enough pressure, he must make O_1 put the dribble down before shooting and also contest the shot off the dribble. Also, X_1 cannot allow O_1 to penetrate into the lane or he has lost containment. Mix up guards on forwards, centers on guards, etc., so that each player learns his own strengths and weaknesses as well as recognizing the same in the player he is defensing.

Defensive Post Denial

The use of two balls in a post denial drill has proven to be challenging and effective in emphasizing this fundamental (Diagrams B and C).

C passes to either wing and X_1 must deny the direct pass to O_1 (start O_1 below X_1 in the lane and have them both facing C.) The wing players must throw a pass within two seconds. As X_1 knocks the first pass away, C picks up the second ball and passes quickly to the opposite wing. X_1 must now deny a second pass to O_1 across the lane. X_1 must keep both passes from being received by O_1. Should O_1 catch either pass, X_1 plays defense on the ball until the play is over.

Box Out

Our favorite drill for this Raider Rule involves having the defensive player make two consecutive effective "box outs" on different players (Diagrams D and E).

X_1 lines up the lane on the dotted line. O_1 and O_2 are at the elbows and O_3 starts with the ball at the top of the key. O_3 passes to either side and coach immediately shoots. X_1 boxes out the offensive player opposite the shooter. (This would be O_1 in Diagram D.) X_1 outlets the ball to O_3 who immediately passes to the remaining offensive player (in this case, O_2). X_1 plays 1-on-1 defense on O_2 and boxes out the shooter. X_1 must get two consecutive rebounds without allowing an offensive rebound or score to get out of the drill (Diagram E).

Offensive Movement without the Ball

The best drill to emphasize moving without the ball is to play 3-on-3 or 4-on-4 half court and not allow the offense to dribble. This maximizes defensive pressure on the ball and forces the offensive players to move constantly in order to set up good scoring opportunities. The offense must score to get out the drill. This does not allow them to take poor shots. Rotate the defensive players if they don't allow a score to reward them

Combination Drills   **133**

for a good effort.

Ballhandling

Again, this is an area that can and should be emphasized in all offensive drills. What we emphasize in ball handling is making good decisions, or making the percentage play. We have found the following two drills put a premium on sound ballhandling.

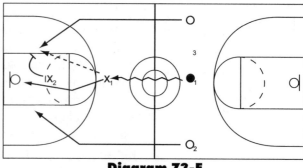

Diagram 73-F

Drill #1 (Diagrams F and G) is the 3-on-2, 2-on-1 full floor conversion drill. Three offensive players (O_1, O_2, O_3) attack two defensive players (X_1, X_2). When X_1 and X_2 gain possession of the ball, they convert offensively to the offensive end of the floor against one of the three offensive players (in this case O_3 who took the first shot). O_1 and O_2 become defensive players for the next group of three offensive players. Since the offense always has a man advantage, they should get a decent shot. We have found that most poor shots or "no shot" situations

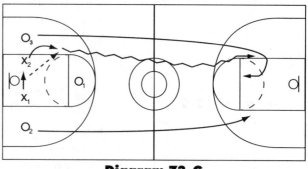

Diagram 73-G

are the result of poor ballhandling decisions. Usually, a mistake is made by a player trying to make an outstanding play rather than an easy play.

In Drill #2 (Diagram H), we play 3-on-4 offense, limiting the offense to play only on the strongside (ball side). We want to pass the ball into the post area, preferably to O_3, but any player may post up. The offense is free to do what they can to open up the post area. The extra defensive player, X_4, may trap, double team, play weakside post defense, etc. This puts extra pressure on the offense to be sound in its ballhandling decisions and strong when catching, passing, or dribbling the ball.

Diagram 73-H

Shoot Good Shots

As with defensive talk, shooting good shots can be stressed in almost all offensive drills. And, as with ball handling, what we emphasize is sound decisions in shot selection. We mentioned before that shooting range, defensive pressure, and game situation are the three factors that determine a good shot for us.

Defensive pressure is fairly subjective since some players have a quicker release, jump higher, etc., on shots, so this can vary from player to player. We feel if

Diagram 73-1

a player had to change something in his basic shot (rush it, arc it higher, lean in one direction or another, always off a dribble, etc.), it was probably not a real good shot in terms of defensive pressure. Likewise, only by practicing different game situations will players learn what we mean by good and bad shots with respect to game situation.

We do use a shooting drill that we believe indicates fairly accurately a player's shooting range. This drill is done early in the season (Diagram I).

We start with a half-court marked off in semi-circles nine feet, fifteen feet, and twenty-one feet from the basket. 0_1 shoots 10 shots within the nine-foot range, rebounding each shot and passing out to 0_2, and then receiving a pass back in a different spot but within the same range. After his 10 shots, 0_1 becomes the passer and 0_2 is the shooter. The pair then advance on out into each range and makes and misses are recorded for each player in each area.

To make the shooting similar to game situations, each player has 30 seconds to shoot ten shots in the nine-foot range, 37 seconds to shoot ten in the middle range, and 45 seconds to shoot ten in the last range. A player must shoot at least ten shots, as any number less than 10 is recorded as a miss. (For example, if a player hits 6 of 9, it would be recorded 6 of 10.) This makes the players shoot quickly, as in games, but they don't have to rush if they hustle between shots.

After a period of time, usually ten days to two weeks, we will have shot a minimum of 100 shots in each area. We believe a player must hit 70 percent of these uncontested shots in an area to be allowed to shoot from that area in live game situations. This has been proven to be a reliable and, more importantly, objective method to determine a player's shooting range. In addition, it has increased each player's concentration and intensity in our shooting drills. A player learns shooting discipline from this as we believe the first step to shoot good shots is to only shoot shots in your range.

Coaching Cues:

Use the basic concepts/principles as your primary coaching cues.

Coach:

Jim Dafler was coaching at Mount Union College (OH) when he wrote this article.

2 vs. 1 — Shot Recognition Drill

Purpose:

To develop proper shot selection – to include not only "how" to shoot, but "when" to shoot. Also, to encourage the development of team play through communication.

Description:

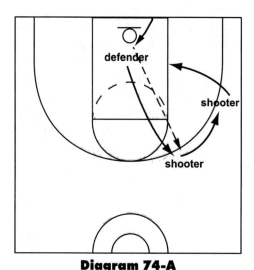

Diagram 74-A

Diagram 74-B

Three players and one coach – 2 offensive players (shooters) and 1 defensive player (shot contester).

Shooters "spot up" with desired spacing and defender mutually aligned in the lane and coach (passer) located under the basket.

Coach controls the drill by choosing to pass to one of the shooters and the defender closes out after seeing the ball. The shooter reads the defense and decides either to shoot or make one more pass to the other shooter. There is a maximum of two passes (to include coach's pass).

Dynamic component of the drill is implemented by the coach verbalizing "right" or "left" and all players rotating (changing offensive and defensive positions) accordingly as quickly as possible.

Coaching Cues:

To be taught both statically (players are standing prior to receiving coach's pass) and dynamically (players have rotated position prior to the coach's initial pass).

Coach should yell "right" or "left" (players' right and left) in order to rotate spots.

Coach controls drill. Example: slower pass allows defender to get to the ball quicker and therefore encourage the second pass, etc.

Players must use verbals – open player must call "ball" to help teammate read the open man and the passer must yell "shot" (early) to the shooter to help him/her read the open shoot.

Coach:

James Seward starts his 11th year at the University of Central Oklahoma helm in 1997-98, bringing a 186-103 record into the season. Has led the Broncos to five Lone Star Conference championships, four NCAA II national tournament appearances, one NCAA II Elite Eight appearance and four NCAA II scoring titles. He is a three-time LSC Coach of the Year honoree. UCO has averaged 21.0 wins a season in the 1990s under Seward, with eight All-Americans and four LSC MVPs. Overall, Seward has 381-262 record in 23 years, with stops at Kansas-Newman, Ashland (OH) and Wayne State (NE). Coach Seward is on the NABC Board of Directors.

Diagram 74-C

DRILL 75

Pressure Workups
Fall '83 Basketball Bulletin

Purpose:

Provide a competitive offensive and defensive drill that has automatic substitution rules for major mistakes.

Description:

What we need is "pressure without problems." We look at this from both an offensive and defensive standpoint. Defensively, the idea is to pressure the heck out of the offense without creating yourself defensive problems. The idea from the offensive standpoint is that offense must become fond of pressure, to the point that fundamentals are still executed in spite of it and offensive objectives are still met. So, the thinking goes, devise a psychological environment in which both offense and defense must put pressure on each other with the objective of breaking the other side down while at the same time learning to concentrate while doing it so as not to get broken down themselves. The idea is "pressure without problems."

Let me go further. Only two things can really foul you up on offense: 1) the big TO (turnover), and 2) the forced shot, which is just another form of TO. If any of those things happen to an offensive player – they're gone from the drill and they lose the privilege and pleasure of having the ball. They go to the end of the line.

Defensively, we think that the worst situation to be in on defense is to have a guy driving the ball to the basket. So, priority number one on defense is not to give up penetration. This is the first rule that we work on when we start the season. Now, at the same time, we are encouraging good, reasonably spaced ball pressure. But getting ball pressure is encouraged by the drill – for without it, the defense will never pressure a TO or a forced shot. The offense is simply playing in too much *psychological comfort* to make a mistake. When the blow-by is being conquered defensively, we add priority number two — hard denials on receivers. Again, this is a pressure concept. If you are on the ball, not getting blown-by, and have teammates in tough denials, the temperature rises. An important part of priority number two is the denial of the lane area to any pass. We emphasize cleanly jarring cutters who want to come across the lane for the ball, or simply post up. If a guy gives up a lane cut — he's gone. Number three priority is a second shot. Second shots mean the defensive player was gone. A number four priority can be added and that would be *talking* on defense. Recently, I saw Paul Landreaux's team from El Camino, playing a summer league game, and I have never seen so much talking by a team in my life, and this was summer. At this point we are not sure what exactly should be said by each position to *avoid being kicked out*. We are playing with the idea that the man who is guarding the ball to should yell *BALL* or the word, *PRESSURE*. If he doesn't, he's back on the bench *(kicked out)*. We are thinking of words like, *HELP LEFT, HELP RIGHT, CLEAR* for people on either side of the ball. People away from the ball checking cutters would use the word, *JAM*. The word, *DENY* wouldn't be so bad also. The word *SHOT* would trigger a block out, etc.

The *pressure workup system* has almost countless advantages. Here are some:

1. It focuses awareness of the best kind. Every day, day after day, your ball players are reminded just how foolish TOs are. Forced shots, too. When they go in a ball game, they have a very clear idea of what's right, what's wrong, and the importance of making good decisions. They are far less likely to try to make some low percentage homerun play that looks great one in ten times and turns it over the other nine.

2. It is competitive in better than gamelike conditions. You'll be putting way more pressure on yourselves than any opponent will – and you will enjoy pressuring opponents into problems and you'll enjoy having opponents fold in an attempt to pressure you into them. It makes discussion of the mental aspects of a great contest so easy. "Look guys, the opponent is pressuring the heck out of you and we're pressuring the heck out of them." Now, who is going *to lean their will* on it and concentrate harder? Break them down. They start to understand the mind set of playing with objectives and concentrating on them until they are happening.

3. Your best players are going to be practicing plenty of offense and you have a couple of comforting things working for you as the coach. First, you know they wouldn't be on offense unless they were successful on "D," and secondly, if you have a great one who is not staying on offense long enough to satisfy him, then you really have a teaching tool. The point is that despite his greatness, he's hurting you with either TOs or forced shots. Let him be as frustrated as you are. He'll get that way waiting in line.

4. In a way, the thing polices itself. Players begin recognizing blow-bys and take themselves out. Sure as heck the *first* guy in line recognizes it. Besides, you can positively comment and not be negative. The guy who is successful in breaking another guy down into a mistake can get plenty of praise. The drill does an awful lot of your reprimanding for you.

5. It can be done 1-on-1; 2-on-2; 3-on-3; 4-on-4; 5-on-5.

6. We just use our man offense in scrimmage time and put guys on "D" and do it that way by position. Have three lines of subs; posts, wings, and point.

7. In practice, if you have guys that aren't competing very well, they will be in the lines a lot. Won't take much offense to break them down.

There are a lot more advantages. Let me now list some hints for development:

1. After a time, the forwards on defense will get mad because they will deny hard and a guard will make a chance pass to forward and it will TO. The guard will be in good shape because he'll get to be on "O," but the forward gets nothing

for his work. So what I did was to say that to any TO on an entry pass was cause for both offensive guys to get thrown out. Boy, will the offensive forward get mad at a guard for making a bad pass. You won't have to police it. The players take care of it for you.

2. We play a lot of our two-play concepts full-court. We tell the defense that they can take all sorts of chances by putting pressure on the guards because you are making the offense score in the pattern. So, if the "D" can turn them over in the backcourt, throw out the whole *perimeter*. Once it crosses half-court, then it is straight up regular workups. As soon as the play is completed, give the ball back to one of the offensive guards down near the basket and it goes the other way.

3. With as many coaches as you have – you can police it. Emphasize different things on different days. If the "D" is not pressuring the entry leads enough, throw them out. There's a lot you can do and much of it you can do in a friendly sort of way. The drill is the rascal!

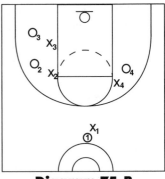

Diagram 75-A

Diagram 75-B

4. *IMPORTANT.* You have to make fast transitions when you make a change. The guys in line are holding shirts in their hands. "D" are skins. If a "D" guy conquers an "O", the guy in line comes on and slaps the shirt on the guy who was "D." If the guy on "O" conquers the guy on "D," the guy coming on just flips the shirt to the guy leaving.

Summary Pressure Workups
<u>Teams</u>: 5-on-5 (Diagram A) or 4-on-4 (Diagram B).
Recommended time per day: 20-30 minutes.
The only way you can get "kicked off" the offensive team:
    1. Turnover
    2. Bad or forced shot.

Note: When you get kicked off you go to the end of the bench and start your workups.
The only way you can get "kicked off" the defense:
    1. *A blow-by* (offensive man drives around you)
    2. Fail to deny lead
    3. Fail to block out
    4. Fail to talk

The only way you can go from defense to offense is:
    1. Force a turnover
    2. Force a bad shot

Coaching Cues:

Provide drill guidelines for 1-on-1, 2-on-2, 3-on-3, 4-on-4, and 5-on-5 competition that automatically substitutes players for "major **OFFENSE & DEFENSE mistakes**" in your system of play. They then go to the back of the substitute line and earn their right to stay on the floor.

Coach:

Gary Colson coached at Pepperdine, New Mexico and Fresno State during a long, successful coaching career.

Station Drills
Fall '83 Basketball Bulletin

Purpose:

Teach players fundamental skills in a drill circuit training organization.

Description:

You won't find many successful coaches, or successful people, whose lives are organized, whose practices aren't organized, whose teams aren't organized. I've spent a great deal of time working with station fundamentals.

It took me a couple of years to realize we could use the station work that we were doing in our camp programs in our own basketball practices, in trying to teach our own offenses or defenses. Station work is the kind of thing you can use for some big men and for some guards, but I use them in a lot of different ways.

Fundamentals are often overlooked. You can have the greatest offense in the world, but if you can't pass the ball or create a pass, your offense is not going to be any good. If you can't do a quick ball reversal, you're not going to score. If you can't screen, you're not going to get open.

There are some basic reasons why you would want to use station fundamentals to begin with:

1. You can teach in a concentrated time period.
2. Compatible players may be placed together, usually three per station.
3. Constant movement prevents boredom.
4. A by-product is conditioning, especially in pre-season.
5. Leadership is promoted among teammates.
6. Utilizes all available space.
7. Allows for breakdown work.
8. Easy to change ineffective stations.

The first thing you determine, before your practice ever starts, is how you want your personnel matched up. I make a practice sheet every day and make sure every player has a copy. We do it all on time. If we have ten minutes set aside for a drill, then we go on to the next one after that time. I think that keeps you from getting yourself in a position where you don't run over on your schedule.

Station work is something you have to wait on. You won't look super at it the first day or two because you'll be, just basically, teaching. First, you have to determine how many kids you're going to involve in your stations. After you've done that, then you determine how many stations you actually want to use. I use seven,

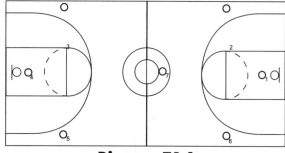

Diagram 76-A

with one floating station and sometimes, two. It doesn't really matter how many stations you have as compared to kids, it just matters how much time you want to spend on it and how many different varieties of things you want to cover. I usually use my station work after stretching, and I believe in stretching with all my heart. Stretching is crucial, and then we do our shooting. After we're good and loose, we do our station work.

Early in the season, I use diversity drills to work on fundamentals. You really can get your assistants involved in fundamental teaching. Use a lot of people. Everybody is busy and nobody is standing around.

Here's a setup relative to a basic diversity of drill work (see Diagram A). Let's say we're going to use seven stations. You can use the middle area as a station if you don't have some extra areas like a stage, or hallway. I'll use these seven drills to start the season.

The very first one is a screening drill. There are so many kids who just can't screen properly. You look to screen on the ball and off the ball. You have to learn to do the job of screening. Make them move to the hole to get the ball, re-set and go again. They're only going to be at this station for minute and a half. (See Diagram B) When you screen off the ball you stress reading the screen properly and setting the screen properly. We all try to stress screening, but here we've isolated it.

Diagram 76-B

The second one I use is just a basic two-on-one passing drill. I really want that defensive man in the middle active for the whole 30 seconds. I want him to try to deflect the pass. Here's one place where you don't even need a basket.

At Station 3, again you don't even need a basket to do the ball handling drills. I give them these guides: Take the ball five times around the right leg, and left leg, waist, head. I start them out slapping the ball five times, as hard as they can, either side. Then we duck-walk in place where they come up and down and take the ball in-between their legs. If we still have time before a minute and a half, we start up and do it all over again.

I really like drill Number 4. This is one place where I think you need a coach if you can. It's what I call my spread-eagle rebounding drill. We put them on the floor in this fashion (shown in Diagram C) to get the good outlet pass. Number 1 throws the ball against the backboard. He goes and gets it as high as he can and comes off with it in the proper rebounding position, spread-eagled, turns outside and makes the two-handed outlet pass to Number 2. He immediately makes a two-handed chest pass across the floor to Number 3. He follows his pass, and #3

Combination Drills   **143**

Diagram 76-C

Diagram 76-D

gives it back to him. Number 1 goes to where #2 was and #3 goes to where #1 was. Number 2 throws it on the board and #3 goes and gets it and throws it to the outlet man.

At Station 5, you need a basket and I call this my Superman drill because the guy is on the fly. You throw the ball over the rim to try to teach them to follow the basketball. They get outside the lane, they throw it over the rim, they go and get it, then they throw it the other way, back and forth. I keep a manager there to keep track of how many times they do it. It's a quickness drill and, also, you're trying to get them into a position to follow the ball. You're trying to make them move.

The big kids really like Station 6. The guards like to call it the "Ram at the Basket" Drill, because they can't dunk. You put a ball on the blocks (shown in Diagram D) and you have an offensive man. The other two men are right underneath the basket. It goes 30 seconds for one man. On the horn, he goes and gets the ball and, if he can dunk it, he dunks it. If he can't dunk it, he picks it up and rams it at the hole as hard as he can. As soon as he lets that ball go, he goes and gets the other ball. The man under the basket picks up the first ball and puts it back on the block. It keeps all three players involved that way. They keep doing it, the offensive players slamming the ball at the hole, the defensive players picking it up and putting the ball back on the blocks. You teach them to be aggressive, to be able to shoot the ball and get the three-point play.

On the seventh station, I have them use the rebounder for 30 seconds each. If you don't have that machine, use a dribble-steal in the middle of the floor. You put a guy in the ring, he dribbles with one hand and tries to steal it with the other. If the ball goes out of the ring, the other guy gets in.

That's the way, over the years, I've developed my stations. I have over 400 of them I've used at my camps.

Coaching Cues:

Emphasize constant movement, selected fundamental work, personal and team leadership, and breakdown drills.

Coach:

Don Lane, longtime head coach of Transylvania University (KY), is a leader in NAIA college circles. He has taken his team to the NAIA national tourney.

DRILL 77

Station Drills

Winter '85 Basketball Bulletin

Purpose:

Teach players fundamentals and conditioning during a skill circuit training program.

Description:

One of the principles that we have followed in practice is to work under game conditions as often as possible. This translates to working under pressure while subjected to physical stress. The pressure in a practice situation may be provided by using a clock, striving for a predetermined goal, or simply by the watchful eye of the coach. Stress comes from exertion and fatigue.

We have found that by using individual stations we can work on any phase of fundamental development and also receive the double benefit of a high intensity conditioning program. In order for the cardio-respiratory system to be in the "training zone" (where efficiency increases) the heart rate should remain between 120-180 beats per minute for a 6-8 minute duration. By using the station approach which follows, our athletes maintained this range for at least eight minutes, depending on what activity they had performed to the stations. Checking the heart rate provides a convenient way to determine which players are working to capacity and which players are not. If one of your players runs through this program and does not get into the 140-170 range, he is not working.

We budget fifteen minutes to this drill, incorporating twelve one-minute stations and allowing 10 seconds between each station. The 10 seconds are the rest or recovery period between each station and are spent going from Station #1 to Station #2, etc. This leaves one minute at the end of the drill (if it went smoothly) to rest before moving on to the next segment of practice. It is essential that the coaching staff is organized and that the stations are planned to coordinate smooth movement from one station to the next. (See Diagram A)

Station #1 (1 minute)-JUMP ROPE

The number of repetitions depends entirely on the proficiency of the athlete. A goal of at least 100 per minute is not too demanding for a fairly good jumper. 10 second-Rotate

Station #2 (1 minute)-DRIBBLING.

We put our player in a jump circle and tell him that there is one minute left in the game and that he must protect the ball using all his dribbling skills while remaining within the circle. We tell him to use his imagination and to be innovative. 10 Second-Rotate

Station #3 (1 minute)-LINE HOPS

Two feet together hopping back and forth over an out-of-bounds line-emphasis should be on quickness and not letting the hips and shoulders rotate. 150 per minute is an easily attainable goal. 10 Second-Rotate

Station #4 (1 minute)-FOUL SHOOTING

A rebounder is needed, at least 6 shots should be taken using the shooter's complete routine – the rebounder must hustle on the miss. 10 Second-Rotate

Station #5 (1 minute)-LINE SLIDES

The player straddles a foul lane – gets in his defensive stance and slides laterally line to line – he does not have to go outside the lane with both feet – points of emphasis are staying down and pointing the lead foot. 10 Second-Rotate

Station #6 (1 minute) - BALL-HANDLING

Single leg circles, double leg circles, hip circles, spider, etc.-at full intensity. 10 Second-Rotate

Station #7 (1 minute)-MIKAN DRILL

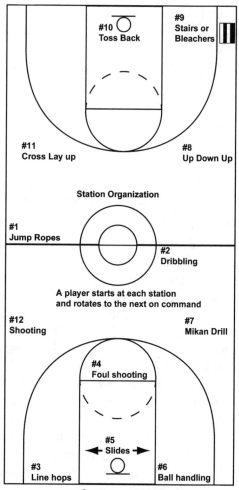

Diagram 77-A

Baby hooks inside the lane – left to right, right to left, etc. – stress, rhythm, follow-through, pivoting, and catching the ball in a shooting position without bringing it down – 30 is good. 10 Second-Rotate

Station#8 (1 minute)-UP-DOWN-UP DRILL

Rebounder tosses the ball up on the glass-goes up high to rebound – comes down keeping the ball up above head and then goes back for the layup, repeats process – 12 per minute is good. 10 Second-Rotate

Station #9 (1 minute)-STAIRS

We were fortunate to have stairs adjoining our gym and our players made the most of them – players must grasp hand rail and push themselves. 10 Second-Rotate

Station #10 (1 minute)-TOSS BACK

We use the toss back in conjunction with a big man move and or passing. An example would be rebound – outlet to toss back – receive on jump stop from toss back – power move to basket – repeat. 10 Second-Rotate

Station #11 (1 minute)-CROSS LAYUP DRILL

Start at the right elbow – dribble in right handed for right handed layup, dribble out to left elbow with the right hand – turn into the ball using the left hand to dribble in to the left hand layup – dribble out left handed to right elbow – turn in using right hand – repeat – emphasis on pushing off pivot foot and protecting ball – 12 per minute is good, 10 Second-Rotate

Station #12 (1 minute)-PERIMETER SHOOTING

A coach or manager rebounds as the shooter constantly moves baseline to baseline around a 15' perimeter – target hand, proper footwork, using the glass between the box and second hash mark are points of emphasis.

In a fifteen minute period of practice, we were able to cover nine fundamentals of basketball, plus associated skills (passing, catching, jumping, etc.), all with intensity. There are many different options to this type of station approach. You may wish to concentrate on a particular skill and thus may wish to repeat a station at some point during the rotation. It is also possible to combine more than one player at a station thus working on two- and three-man skills. The possibilities are endless but the results are the same. You are maximizing your practice efficiency by providing your players an enjoyable, but demanding program to improve fundamentals and conditioning.

Coaching Cues:

Coaches can circulate to cover all stations. Stations can be selected to cover any fundamentals coaches may want to emphasize. In 15 minutes 12 stations can be covered.

Coach:

Lee Talbot was an assistant coach at East Carolina University when he wrote this article.

DRILL

78

Motivation by Drills
Spring '83 Basketball Bulletin

Purpose:

Teach players to motivate themselves using drills that are challenging and fun.

Description:

If you have been in this business very long, you must have a loud voice. If you do not have a loud voice, you're in trouble. I yell!

Personality plays an important part in motivation. If you do not have the personality, you're not going to be able to motivate your kids. When they come over to the bench, you're not going to be able to tell them anything. If you are the one who cannot get things across, then you're going to be in trouble. How do we do that? What we like to do, is we like to do it with drills. Our practice is fun. It's hard, but it's fun. We want them to work, we practice anywhere from an hour and a half to two hours pre-season. No more than an hour and a half after the season starts. Our practice schedule is set up in such a way that everything is moving, competitive.

Ball Handling

When we come out on the floor, we spend 4 or 5 minutes on this drill. Everybody gets a partner and a ball and we warm up with ball handling drills. Slap the ball, bring it around the waist between the legs, what ever they want to do with it. Make them get going, be lively. Make them get loose. You're moving every muscle in your body, it's a great way to get loose. Then we get a rope and jump rope. Now they're really loose.

Baskets (Diagram A)

1. Every basket has 4 players.
2. Passing – Chest pass bam bam pass it around. Reverse it, go the other way. Bounce pass, reach around pass, reverse it.
3. Pressure Lay-ups – One man is offense and one man is defense. Shoot right handed and left handed lay-ups with pressure on the offense. Defense does not block the shot.
4. Bank Shots – Defense cuts the offense off, offense shoots a short bank shot. Defense blocks out after the shot. Then you switch sides of the court, then switch partners.
5. On The Fly – One man throws the ball up on the board, gets the rebound, keeps his elbows straight and puts the ball right back up and in. He does all of

Diagram 78-A

this while in the air. Do the same on the left side. The length of the drill is 1-1½ minutes.

6. Back To The Floor – This drill has given us more points in basketball games than any other drill. Throw the ball up on the board. Go get the ball, elbows straight, without bringing the ball down, shoot it in the basket.

7. Defensive Throw-out – Same four people will be at the same basket all week. One man will throw it out to his partner, the outlet man.

8. Free throws – Everybody shoots 10 free throws. They have to make 7 out of 10. If they don't make 7 out of 10 on Monday, they stay after practice and shoot 50. If they don't make 7 out of 10 on Tuesday, they stay after practice and shoot 100. If they don't make 7 out 10 on Wednesday, same kid, they stay after practice and shoot 500.

Sometimes we go baskets at the end of practice. We do this to shoot free throws when we are tired.

Guard Drills (Diagram B)

1. The coach rolls the ball out from underneath the basket. Somewhere along the line the coach blows the whistle.
2. Each guard will dive or sprint to the ball.
3. The guard that gets it comes back and scores.
4. The guard that doesn't get it stops the other from scoring.
5. If the offense scores, the defense runs two sprints immediately.

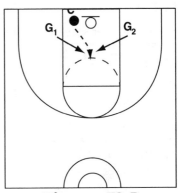

Diagram 78-B

Two Ball Drill (Diagram C)

1. The offensive man tries to get open to receive a pass from the coach.
2. Defense denies the man the ball.
3. When the offense gets open, the coach passes him the ball. Immediately the manager passes the other ball to the coach.
4. Offensive man and defensive man play 1-on-1 knock down drag out. We don't call any fouls.
5. Once the shot is gone, they forget the first ball, and play another ball.
6. The defensive man must always be ready to play defense again.

Diagram 78-C

Combination Drills   **149**

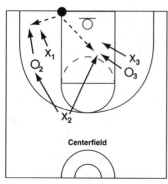

Centerfield

Diagram 78-D

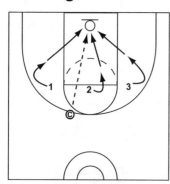

Diagram 78-E

Diagram 78-F

Diagram 78-G

Five Defense – Complete Denial (Diagram D)

1. This drill is for guards and forwards.

2. Do not let the ball come in.

3. If the ball gets in, make the defense go again.

4. No one guards the man out of bounds.

Big Man Drills

1. Slap the Rim – With the ball held firmly by both hands, the big man jumps up and slaps the rim with the ball. Do it over and over again. It makes them learn to hold on to the ball. For smaller men, slap the board.

Superman Drill (Diagram E)

1. Throw the ball high on the board. Run across the lane and catch it.

2. Throw back, make them do it six times. Have another man ready to go next.

Three-On-None (Diagram F)

1. The coach has the ball. He throws the ball at either side of the bankboard or over the basket.

2. Every person is facing the coach.

3. When the ball is shot, the coach yells "shot."

4. The middle man is on his own, he turns any way he wants to. The 2 outside players must turn to the outside, then go for the ball, hard!

5. Whoever gets the rebound, does not break his elbows, and puts the ball in. The other players play defense by trying to block the shot. We will blow a quick whistle if the ball hits the floor. Don't let them fight for it on the floor, keep the ball up.

6. The main purpose of the drill is to teach our players to go for the ball, keep the ball up, and power it up and in.

Save the Ball (Diagram G)

1. The coach rolls the ball out of bounds. It could also be a lob or a bounce pass.

2. The closest player runs to save the ball and throws it back in.

3. Everybody talks. When player 3 runs for the ball, player 2 is taking a route to either side of the ball, yelling, here I am, throw it here.

4. As soon as 2 gets the ball, he throws it back to the coach and the coach throws it to 1 on the other side.

The **NABC** Drill Book

5. The coach may also throw a high lob to the baseline and the middle man will go after it and throw it back in.

6. We even try to save the ball on the other team's end of the floor.

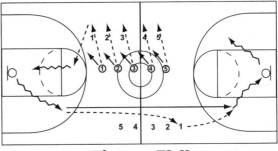

Diagram 78-H

We substitute this drill instead of running sprints. It's like a chinese fire drill (Diagram H).

1. Line up 5 players in the middle of the floor, each with a ball. Number them from 1-5.

2. Line up 5 players on the right side of the court. Number them 1-5.

3. Line up 5 players on the left side of the court. Number them 5-1.

4. Ones are together, they are partners. So are 2's, 3's, 4's, and 5's.

5. Put 1 minute on the clock.

6. Number 1 passes to right Number 1 and gets a return pass.

7. Number 1 dribbles to the foul line and shoots.

8. He gets the rebound, and on the dribble passes the ball to left Number I at the other end.

9. He gets the ball back, shoots above the free throw line, rebounds and passes the ball to Number 1 again.

10. It can be a long pass or a short pass, but he must pass and receive it back before he can shoot.

11. All five go at once!! It's wild, but it's fun.

12. It's important that everyone knows their partner.

13. Have a coach or manager at each end counting the number of baskets made in 60 seconds.

14. Switch groups. Bring in new group to the middle.

15. After all three groups have gone, have them go again. Tell them that they must make more baskets than they did before. If not, go again.

16. This motivates kids to work harder to score more.

17. End your practice on a good note. Tell them if they beat their record, they can go in early.

<u>Tip the Ball and Run (Diagram I)</u>

1. Number 1 and Number 6 have a ball. They throw the ball on board, and the next person in line must tip the ball back to the board.

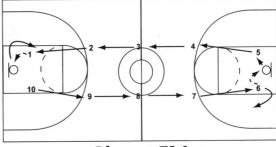

Diagram 78-I

2. It's a great conditioner as well as a ballhandling drill.

3. If you do it one day with 6 on each side, do it the next day with 5.

All of our drills are 2-on-2, 3-on-3, 4-on-4. We very rarely work 5-on-5. Our kids love to scrimmage, but we seldom do.

Coaching Cues:

Enthusiasm is catching – be a carrier. Make each drill challenging and fun. Work hard and keep everyone moving.

Coach:

Tom Creamer was the head coach at Shelby County High School (KY) when he wrote this article.

DRILL 79

Aggressiveness Drills
Winter '78 Basketball Bulletin

Purpose:

Teach players how to develop aggressiveness with specific drills.

Description:

Aggressiveness as defined by the speaker is that of being under control but not violent. This trait is less prevalent in women athletes than it is in men. It is my feeling that you can develop aggressiveness through drills and by the coach showing these tendencies as well. Usually the gifted athlete is the one that needs the help. The average athlete usually has this, because without it, they cannot be successful.

Why are athletes not aggressive? One of the reasons is that it is a role conflict. Their family background has been such that they have been taught not to be aggressive. Many players also fear the possibility of being injured. A third reason is that their own individual personality is not suited towards aggression.

What we talk about as far as aggressiveness is concerned are two things – mental and physical toughness. There are three definite steps in the development of aggressiveness: 1) Set specific goals. Do this for your total team, as well as for an individual. What is very important in each of your goals is that they are measurable. Getting loose balls, taking the charge, etc. 2) Give positive feedback when aggressive behavior comes forth. It is critical that the coach identifies new, aggressive behavior and rewards the player each time. 3) Tell and show players what you want in terms of aggressive behavior. It is important that you show them that it is necessary to be aggressive before they can be successful. Many times you must use force to get your own way. Later on, your players then will look forward to a tough challenge, in the form of an opponent or in a particular game situation.

What is mental toughness? 1) It is an attitude. 2) You must be strong minded and under control at all times. 3) It is nothing more than self discipline. Mental fatigue usually occurs before physical fatigue. Players must realize this, and try to overcome this fatigue factor. Another trait that is necessary for mental toughness is to be emotionally stable. This means having the ability to work long and hard on skills under mental and physical adversities. We use 15 drills in developing aggressiveness (mental and physical toughness).

1. <u>Killer</u> (see Diagram A). This is a one-on-one game to 5 baskets with minimal rules. They are: You can use any body part to stop the player from scoring, except the hands. Rules may be adaptable, depending upon your situation.

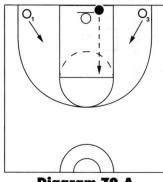

Diagram 79-A

Diagram 79-B

Diagram 79-C

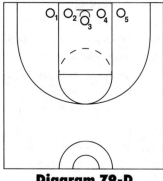

Diagram 79-D

After you score, you do not need to clear the ball, you can just keep scoring one basket after the other. To start the game the players will line up on the baseline, the coach will be between the two players, and the ball will be rolled towards the foul line. The coach will say "go" any time he/she wishes, letting the ball go towards the foul line, top of the key, or even further. It is now one-on-one until five baskets have been scored by one player.

Killer Rules:

A. 1-on-1, 5 baskets

B. Only rule – No use of hands

C. Need not clear on made basket

D. Coach rolls ball and yells "go" for players to fight for ball possession

2. Suicide (see Figure B). Three players play to three baskets. The players are usually a post man, a small guard, and your meanest forward. Same rules as "Killer". As soon as someone scores three baskets, the winner gets a drink, and the other two players play "Killer".

Suicide Rules:

A. 3 players to 3 baskets

B. Same rules as Killer

C. Winner leaves, losers play Killer

3. Football. Whole team plays. One ball is used, and they can use any basket on the court. Again, the only rule is that no hands can be used. When one team scores, the game is over.

4. 30-Second Loose Ball (Figure C). Starts the same way as "Killer". When a player gets possession, he/she is ahead by one point, and there are 30 seconds left in the game. Defensive player must now decide when to foul, or when to try for the steal. If fouled, the offensive player then goes to the foul line to shoot one-and-one.

30-Second Loose Ball Rules:

A. Starts like Killer

B. Offensive player is ahead by 1 with 30 seconds left

C. Defense must try to steal ball or foul at best time

5. 5 Players, 4 Balls (See Figure D). Four balls are lined up at the foul line; five players line up at the baseline. At the signal, players try to gain possession of the four balls. The person without the ball must now try to steal it from the other players dribbling their ball. Failing, he/she must go to the floor to get the ball. When the offensive player loses the ball, they will now go on defense. A 30-second time limit is used. The players must stay within the half court area. Good ballhandling drill, as well as defensive drill to steal the ball. Then it goes to 5-on-3, 5-on-2, and 5-on-1, with the same rules.

Diagram 79-E

Five Players and 4 Balls Rules:

A. Player without ball tries to steal ball from other 4 players for 30 seconds

B. Players must remain in half court

C. When you lose ball, you're on defense

D. No fouling

E. Remove 1 ball and play 5-on-3, then 5-on-2 and 5-on-1.

Diagram 79-F

6. Score on Rebound and Shoot Through Arms. The offensive player takes the ball off the floor, and shoots through the arms of two players that are placed above the offensive player in relaxed position.

7. Pick on the Post (see Figure E). Post man lines up at side post. Each player on the team lines up in a straight line, away from the post man and plays one-on-one. Post man must stop *everybody* on the team from scoring. As soon as someone scores, it starts over. There are no rules.

8. War on the Boards. This is a block off drill. Five players on defense and five players on offense, the coach is shooting. Each player must aggressively keep the offensive player off the boards. If the offensive team gets the ball, the defense must spring down to the opposite baseline and back. Do for 5 minutes. One addition would be to have the ball bounce once before the defense can gain control.

9. Circle Block-Off. Ball is put in the middle of key, five defensive players must keep five offensive players form getting the ball for a five-second interval.

10. Butting Champ. Two players in a jump circle, butt to butt, game is over when one player is pushed out of the circle.

11. Take the Charge (see Figure F). One-on-one situation and defensive player must take the charge when the offensive player is dribbling up and down the court.

Take the Charge Rules:

A. 1-on-1.

B. Defense must take charge as offense dribbles down court

C. Learning to take the blow and recover quickly

12. <u>One-on-one</u>. Definite rules are given, the coach will officiate and try to get the best matchups among his squad members.

13. <u>Two-on-Two</u>. Same as #12 above, best squad matchups.

14. <u>Stutter Step</u>. The player yells his name and stomps his feet on a given signal. This is to help talking on defense and increase his ability to be aggressive.

Coaching Cues:

Develop aggressiveness by setting specific goals, reinforce aggressive behavior, tell and show players what is expected, and relate aggressiveness to success.

Coach:

Cathy Bennedetto is the former women's basketball coach at Seattle University, whose teams were always noted for their aggressive play.

DRILL 80

Keys to Developing Team Strength
Spring '86 Basketball Bulletin

Purpose:

Teach players how to use mental drills to develop individual and team strengths.

Description:

During the course of the past eleven years the author has served as a basketball coach, from the junior high to college level, and incorporated three keys to developing strength and unity within the team. A basketball season covers many days, practices, and games. During this time most teams experience many ups and downs. These three keys to developing team strength will help keep the team on a positive note throughout the season. It is important to note that these keys must be done on a daily basis. It is also important to note that these keys must also be followed before and after games, with some modification, which will be mentioned later. During the author's three year tenure as a high school coach, one of the main reasons for the improvement of a record from 3-18 to 13-8 to 17-5 was the incorporation of these keys into the daily practices. Many of the concepts and ideas in this article come from the author's association during the past six years with Mr. Stan Kellner, author of the book *Taking It To The Limit With Basketball Cybernetics*. The author is fortunate to have shared his friendship over the years, and as a result am able to share these keys with you.

Key Number #1

Key number one involves turning a weakness into a strength. All people have strengths as well as weaknesses in virtually every area of their life. Basketball players tend to hide from their weaknesses and only play to their strengths, thus very few players make a conscious effort to turn a weakness into a strength.

The first step to turning a weakness into a strength is to admit to yourself that you have the weakness. Secondly, you must be willing to admit it to others that you are going to work to improve it.

At the start of each practice all players all players on the team will form a circle. After the coach has made any announcements and/or instructions, each player will state a weakness that he has. Encourage the players to state a specific weakness, i.e., guarding the dribbler, passing to the post, and also encourage players to state a weakness for offense and for defense. When each player has stated his weakness, the coach may wish to state a weakness as a coach that they need to work on. Then regular practice may begin.

It is important that members of the team, and especially the coach, encourage players whenever they play to their weakness during the course of practice. Whether or not the player is successful in playing the weakness is not important. Basically the reason the player has the weakness is that he/she is afraid he/she might fail. Therefore, in order for improvement to occur the player must not be overly concerned with the end result. Remember, encourage the player for playing the weakness, without passing judgement on it. In this manner the player will gain confidence in himself and in his ability to overcome the weakness. The only way to change a weakness into a strength, after all, is to practice it over and over again.

Key Number #2

The second key to developing team strength occurs at the end of each practice. This key involves players and coaches recognizing the good done in a particular practice by a particular player. When practice is finished the team forms a circle. When the coach is finished with any remarks, he/she selects one player to be in the center of the circle. The coach selects a different player each practice until all have gone, and then repeats. The coach, after taking a place in the circle, shouts the player's first name and the entire team shouts the player's last name. This is done three times. The coach then shakes the hand of the player and makes a positive comment about his/her play that particular day in practice. After the coach has gone, each player in turn, shakes the hand and makes a positive comment. It is important to make comments that are somewhat specific (great job on the defensive boards today!) (super shooting from outside today...).

Through this activity the team becomes closer. Certainly all people enjoy giving and receiving compliments. A tremendous sense of team spirit and togetherness is gained through this activity. The player in the center feels special and appreciated by his/her teammates, whether they be a starter or substitute. The person giving the compliment is encouraged to think of something different that has not already been said, therefore a well thought out compliment is usually given. In addition, regardless of the quality of a particular practice, it will always end on a positive note. The more that players are complimented and encouraged, the better they will feel about themselves. The better a player feels about themself the more likely their performance will improve. This is one activity where all players will feel appreciated of their efforts, and will help keep a team together through good and bad times.

Key Number #3

The third and final key to developing team and individual strength is by the setting of goals by individual players. Research by psychologists tells us that only about 10% of the population actively set goals. The goals that a player sets should be selected by the players; however, it is necessary to demand that they do in fact set goals. Each player is asked each Monday to set two goals for the following week, one in the academic area, and one for basketball. The athlete signs the goal card to indicate a promise that he/she has made to themself. The deadline will always be the next Monday. The actual goal should be 3, 4, or 5 words and should be specific, realistic, and easily measurable. On the reverse of the card are the words "WHAT HAVE YOU DONE TODAY TO ACCOMPLISH THIS GOAL." Players are encouraged to keep the goal card in a place where they will see it often, and to make sure that they do in fact do something each day to ensure that they will reach their goal.

At times during the course of the week the coach may wish to compliment the player on a one to one basis for working to achieve the goal or simply ask the player how he is doing in progressing toward the goal. This lets the player know that we as coaches are interested in them as individuals, and take special interest in their quest to achieve goals.

The following Monday all players must present their two goal cards to the coach upon entering the gym. The coach will then ask the player if he/she feels that they have attained the goals. Most times the goal will have been attained, and if this is the case, the coach will place a large W on the card. This is to signify a win, a success, that the goal has been met. The thinking here is that each time a player accomplishes a goal, he is a winner in that sense. The more goals that are achieved, the more wins a player has. This process teaches players that by achieving small goals they are developing the ability to achieve large goals.

In cases where the player does not feel that he/she has reached a goal, a brief conference is in order. This need only takes a minute or so. First of all the player must be reminded that because they did not reach the goals, they are not a failure. Congratulate the player for setting the goals, for charting a path to success. Let them know that there are reasons why people do not achieve goals. Maybe the goal was too high, maybe the player did not really put in the necessary time and effort to accomplish the goal. Most often the player will know why they did not reach the goal. Keep the player's card but do not put a W on it, rather put a LE, to stand for learning experience. Keep positive with the athlete and hand them another goal card for the following week. The athlete then selects a goal they wish to accomplish.

Should an athlete not reach a goal, they do not have to select the same goal week after week. In order for goal settings to be effective the athlete must set a goal that they wish to achieve, not one someone else has told them to do, or one they may have failed at.

After 4-6 weeks, take all the goal cards you have accumulated for each player and staple them together. Pass them out to each payer, and let them review the steps they have taken to become a better student and player. They are developing their own personal tradition of winning.

As coaches we must concentrate our efforts on the improvement and development of the individuals that make up our team. We must be conscious of their improvement as students and as players. Certainly we are also interested in the improvement and development of our team. If a coach will follow the suggestions outlined in this article he/she will be able to chart the progress of individual players. The team will be closer together and supportive of each other, and most important – will recognize each player for their own unique contribution to the team.

It has been said that a basketball season is like a book, and that each game (and the practices leading up to that game) are like a chapter in that book. These keys will keep a team thinking positive, working for improvement and striving to reach goals. One of the best compliments a coach can receive is about the continued improvements of his/her team as the season progresses. These keys may help you close the gap between where you are now, and where you want to be!

Modification For Games

KEY 1. In the locker room before the game, the coach has the team form an informal circle. Each player is asked to make a positive statement in regards to their using weakness in the game, i.e., I will aggressively crash the defensive boards, I will turn the dribbler to his weak hand, I will pass to the post whenever he is open, etc.

KEY 2. After the game the team forms a circle. Start with one player, maybe the captain, and he turns to the player on his right and makes a positive compliment about the offensive play of that player during the game. The player receives that compliment then turns to his right and does same thing, until the player who gave the first compliment receives his. Then the first player who started turns to player on his left and makes a compliment about the defensive plays of that particular player. This is done until the player who started, once again receives a compliment. In the case of a player receiving a compliment who did not play in the game, encourage players to give a compliment about player(s) work in practice that helped the team prepare for the game.

It is the author's belief that the incorporation of these three keys into a daily program will allow a team to experience a feeling of togetherness unique in sports. As coaches we do not only prepare our student-athletes for a season, we prepare them for a lifetime. The lessons of turning a weakness into a strength, giving and receiving compliments, and goal setting will help prepare them for the many challenges they will face through their lifetime.

Keys to Remember

1. Turning a weakness into a strength.
2. Complimenting the work of a particular player(s).
3. The setting of goals.

Coaching Cues:

Focus on the mental drills and three keys: recognize weaknesses and change into strengths, develop team cohesion by reinforcing positive skills/behaviors and set individual and team goals.

Coach:

Michael Larose was assistant to Ron Slaymaker, longtime coach at Emporia State University (KS), where his teams were consistently solid in all phases of the game.

Big Man Drills
Summer '85 NABC Bulletin

Purpose:

Develop individual skills of the post player.

Description:

In the development of the post player, there are three areas to work on:

1. Philosophical – has to do with personal beliefs and the philosophy you believe in, and how you look at post play.
2. Psychological – is the mental approach to post play, and preparation you might have prior to it.
3. Physiological – deals with the technical and physical development and preparation of them towards the post player.

When mentally preparing the post player, several things should be kept in mind:

- Self-image, which is the most important. The coach should talk to the post player one-on-one all the time.
   a. Fear of failure
   b. Lack of self-confidence
   c. Self-consciousness
   d. Poor concentration
   e. Self-condemnation
   f. Anger and frustration
- Everyone must set goals – they should be short range.
- Personal accomplishments boost their ego.
- Coaching assets and strengths.
- Personal qualities you'd like them to change.
- Obstacles that slow the process.

There are physical and tactical parts to the development of the post.

- Stretching – the bigger the post player, the more the need of stretching.
- Body strength – weights for upper body Monday & Thursday, and for lower, Tuesday & Friday during pre-season. During the season, lift twice a week.
- Conditioning – agility drills.
   a. 30-second drill; shuffle back and forth with one foot touching outside the lane.
   b. Half-court, run and stop, obtain defensive stance from pivot stops.

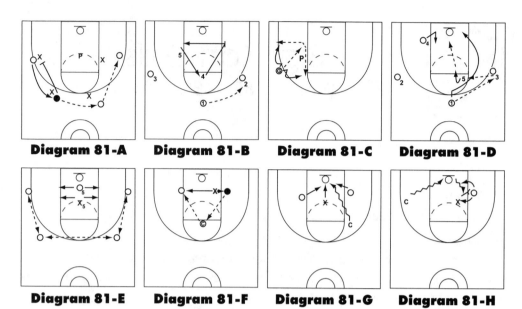

Diagram 81-A **Diagram 81-B** **Diagram 81-C** **Diagram 81-D**

Diagram 81-E **Diagram 81-F** **Diagram 81-G** **Diagram 81-H**

c. Toughness drill – with hands up, give a shot in the chest with football dummy.

d. Loose ball drill – roll the ball from baseline to free throw line, get the possession first and then go 1-on-1.

e. Jumping – boxes for jumping up and down, jumping over string tied between two chairs for two minutes.

Post Players Drills

4-on-4 Shell Drill (Figure A)

Here, the post is without an opponent but is inside talking/encouraging his teammates about screens and cuts and becoming aware of defensive help situations.

Triangle Passing Drill (Figure B)

This drill is for reverse post player movement, to teach anticipation of the pass.

Guard-Post Shooting Drill (Figure C)

The guard throws the ball to the post, cuts either way, and gets the return pass for the shot.

Hi-Low Passing Drill (Figure D)

UCLA guard rub option with hi-low feed passing.

4-on-1 Drill (Figure E)

Good hands up defensive position in the paint with no 3-second calls.

Help and Recover Drill (Figure F)

With two balls, coach passes to players trying to get open in the paint, where they must shoot after good 2-hand catch.

2-on-1 Rebounding Drill (Figure G)

Coach shoots the ball off the glass, and the offense tries to get the rebound, but can't dribble. The goal is to score three offensive rebound baskets. Work as hard as you can to jump as high as you can under control.

Off-Side Rebounding Drill (Figure H)

Offensive player fakes to the outside then springs inside for the tip. He has to read the defense.

Diagram 81-I

Six Must Post Moves (Figure I)

1. Drop-step power layup.
2. Short hook shot.
3. Turn-around jump shot.
4. Spin/ Pull through.
5. Flashing series – using screens.
6. Free Throws – confidence.

5-on-1 Drill (Figure J)

Five players surround the post. The post has to leap to catch the lob pass and then protect it for 10 seconds using pivots, etc.

Diagram 81-J

Coaching Cues:

Focus on physical, tactical and psychological development of your post players.

Coach:

Dave Bliss is a former assistant to Hall of Fame Coach Bob Knight and now has established a very successful program at the University of New Mexico. His Lobos are perennial contenders for the Western Athletic Conference title and for a postseason tournament berth.

Pre-Season Conditioning
Spring '87 Basketball Bulletin

Purpose:

Provide players an organized aerobic and anaerobic cardiovascular program, muscular fitness, and flexibility conditioning program. This program is carried out on land and water and is specifically designed to minimize repetitive impacts on floor surfaces, while achieving maximum overall condition.

Description:

The University of Wisconsin-Platteville pre-season conditioning program has taken shape over our past seasons here. The improvement of our record during this time is a direct reflection of this program. Our players are certainly over-achievers and place a great deal of pride and hard work into these daily workouts. To further prove our point, our players came out with excellent scores when evaluated by the University of Wisconsin-Madison Sports Medicine Clinic.

The information in this article explains in detail the exact layout of the conditioning from September 3 to October 13. We alternate between agilities/games/weights/and aqua-dynamics/hill to provide a wide range of activities that are beneficial aerobically and anaerobically, besides being fun. This diversity also emphasizes different body parts as well.

Our stretching program begins and ends every practice session, both pre-season and regular season. Team flexibility has been improved as well as a reduction in nagging injuries such as muscle pulls.

Finally, to follow NCAA guidelines, basketballs may not be used at any point during the conditioning program when coaches are present. When the gym is used (since we have no indoor track facility), the baskets are raised. The captains select the teams for the pick-up games.

Pioneer Basketball Weight Training

The Universal equipment should be used with a 1-2 positive to negative ratio. This means that the positive force, or push, should be about one-half as long as the negative force, or return of the weight. It's important to note that the working weight should never "bounce" on the weight stack until the complete number of repetitions are obtained. The 8-12 repetition set should be used. This means when a set can be completed with 12 repetitions, the next higher weight should be used until that set reaches 12 repetitions.

Bench Press

The bench press primarily works on the chest muscles. The wider the grip, the more the chest is involved. The secondary muscles involved are the tricep and the front of the shoulder. To emphasize the tricep and shoulder a narrow grip should be used. This machine utilizes progressive resistance, in other words, as the arms extend the resistance increases. This is a definite advantage over the free weights. Also, the feet should be placed on a bench or stool at the same height as the lifting bench to avoid stress on the lower back.

Butterfly

The butterfly works the complete chest. The key to this lift is to use the forearms and to slowly return the weight back down. The upper arm should be parallel to the floor for maximum benefit. More effort should be applied to push the weight at the elbows rather than the hands.

Lateral Pull-Downs

The lateral pull-downs work on the back muscles; when bringing the lat bar to the top of the chest, the lower back is emphasized. Pulling the bar to the back of the neck works on the upper back and the rear shoulder area. Secondary muscles involved are the upper chest and bicep muscles.

Preacher Curls

The preacher curls work the total bicep muscle. Secondary muscle involved is the forearm. The key here is to slowly lower the bar to full extension while keeping the elbows stationary on the pad.

Tricep Extension (use lat pull down bar)

The tricep extension works the complete tri muscle. The key to this lift is to keep the elbows in and extend the wrists downward. Do not swing the bar above the chest area. Once again move to bar down slowly keeping control at all times.

Long Pull

The long pull works the total shoulder area. When pulling the weight upward, towards the ear, the back to the shoulder is emphasized. Bringing the weight back down to hips works on the lats. The key to this lift is to attain the proper circular motion maintaining control of the weight at all times. Start with palms out and end palms in.

Squat

The squat is easily the best total leg lift. When done properly, all muscles of the leg are worked. The main emphasis is the quadriceps and calf muscles. The secondary emphasis are the hamstrings and are worked when the proper depth is attained. The key to the lift is to lower the bar until the hams are at least parallel to the floor, then quickly burst upward. Do not lock knees at any time during the lift.

Leg Extension

The leg extensions work the quadricep muscle. The key here is to hold the locked position for a count, then slowly allow the weight down. Always be in control of the weight.

Leg Curl

The hamstring is the primary muscle. Once again, hold the weight in the farthest upright position, then slowly bring the weight back down.

Total Hip

The key to this lift is lining the working hip with the center of the cam on the machine. Always push the lift out to at least a 90-degree angle. Adduction is pushing out with the resistance on the outside of the leg, and abduction is with the resistance on the inside of the leg. Flexion is achieved by bringing the knee to the chin; an extension is used when extending leg behind the back. Range of motion should be utilized at all times. Make sure the pad is above the knee to avoid any stress on the knee joint.

Sit-Ups

The sit-up should be performed with the knees bent. The shoulders should never touch the board with the furthest extension being just before the chest hits the knees. Never extend fully to avoid a rest situation. The abdominals are emphasized.

Back Extensions

Lock the legs at an even level with the seat. Hips should be placed just over the end of the seat. Hands should be located behind the head. The motion should be down to a 90 degree angle and full extension should NEVER be further than even with the legs.

The "Quality" of the lift (technique) is much more important than the "Quantity" of the lift!

Pioneer Aqua Dynamics

The main purpose of the Pioneer Aqua Dynamic program is to reduce bone/joint stress commonly found in dryland exercises such as sprints, jump-roping and plyometrics. (Our jump-roping and plyometrics are done on surfaces which reduce the stress to joints.) Our Aqua Dynamic program allows us to continue anaerobic development without the added stress to the various parts of the leg.

Exercises done in chest deep water eliminates 80-90 percent of body weight normally found in dryland exercises. Less weight means less joint stress. Also, due to decreased gravitational pull, a greater range of motion and flexibility can be achieved.

One benefit of Aqua Dynamics is the added resistance water creates. For instance, a sprint in water not only eliminates the pounding on the leg, it adds resistance as the legs pass through the water. So you are not only increasing anaerobic threshold, you are increasing overall strength as well.

The Exercises

Exercises should be performed in chest high water to achieve maximum water resistance with minimum body weight.

Cross Pool Sprints. The idea here is to imitate dryland sprints as closely as possible while eliminating arm action. Arms should be held out of the water to increase leg work and decrease the likelihood of helping yourself along with your hands. Emphasis is on the use of a medium stride coupled with the bulk of the stress being placed on the balls of the feet. Distances should be comparable to dryland sprints. For most pools, this will probably mean more than one time back and forth. A 30 yd. sprint will take between 14 and 18 seconds. Maximum effort with as little rest between sets will create the greatest gains.

Cross Pool Cariocas. Once again the dryland carioca should be simulated and once again, arms should be held out of the water. Emphasis should be placed on proper leg follow-through. This is excellent for strengthening hip muscles as well as increasing flexibility.

High Knee Jumps. For this exercise, waist/stomach high water is used. Once again the arms should be held out of the water. The players involved are to bring the knee completely out of the water (ideally up to the chest), return the leg to the pool bottom with the opposite leg beginning the action before the first leg completes. This works the quick jumping muscles of the leg with added resistance and without joint stress. Sets with between 50-100 repetitions with a minimum of rest will create maximum gains.

Power Drives. For this one, water over the head is desired. This is by far the most difficult since both legs and arms are being used. The objectives during power drives are to move the legs with an upright sprinting motion while driving the arms up and down. Both actions are maintained at full intensity with closed hands being used to avoid paddling. This is one of the best (and most difficult) anaerobic development exercises. Sets should last between 45 seconds and one minute, with no more than 30 seconds of rest intervals, in order to achieve maximum gains.

Sample Workout

- Cross Pool Sprints – 30 yds., 60 yds., 90 yds., one of each Cross Pool Cariocas-same as above
- High knee Jumps – three sets of 70 with 30 sec. rest intervals
- Power Drives – three sets of 1 minute with 30 sec. rest intervals.

DRILL 83

Agility Drills

Purpose:

Teach players basketball footwork, balance, and quickness.

Description:

Basketball agility drills are usually done in the off-season and should carefully duplicate the footwork/moves used in basketball. This sample program is done two days per week for twelve weeks, as follows:

Agility Drill Days

Start weeks 8+9 with 3 reps at each agility, with a 20-second rest between each drill; week 8, #1-4; wk 9, #5-8. Do on day listed before interval workout.

Weeks 10+11, do 4 reps at each agility drill with a 15-second rest. Do #8-12

Week 12, do 5 reps at each agility drill with a 10-second rest. Do #'s 2, 5, 7, 8, 12

1. Star Drill: Start with a 10-yard square (10 yards on each side). Start in the middle of the square, first backpedal 5 yards, then sprint back to the start. Next backpedal in a 45 degree angle 5 yards to either the left or right corner, then sprint back to the start. Next do the same to the other corner. Then side-shuffle to the left or the right 5 yards, then sprint back to the start, then do the same to the other side. Next, sprint forward 5 yards, then backpedal back to the start. Next, sprint in a 45 degree angle to either the left or right corner, then backpedal to the start.

2. Reverse 7: Start with 3 cones in the shape of a reverse 7, at 5 yards apart. Sprint up 5 yards to #2 then sprint back to the start, then sprint to and around the far cone, past #2 to #3, then sprint back to the start.

3. Box Drill (7-yard box): Start with a 7-yard square. At the start backpedal 7 yards, at the cone then shuffle 7 yards. At the next cone sprint forward 7 yards. Then at the next cone shuffle back to the start.

4. Box Drill (10-yard box): Start with a 10 yard square. At the start backpedal 10 yards, at the cone carioca 10 yards to the next cone, then sprint 10 yards to the next cone. Then carioca back to the start.

5. Z-Pattern: Arrange cones 15 yards apart by 5 yards north and south (6 cones total).

6. Lateral Shuffle: Set cone 5 yards apart. Put them in 7 rows by 2 yards north and south

7. S-Pattern: Start with 4 cones 7-10 yards apart, 3- 4 yards north to south.

8. X-Pattern: Start with a 5-yard square. At the start backpedal 5 yards then sprint forward at a 45-degree angle toward the far cone. At the cone then backpedal at a 45 degree angle back to the start.

9. I-Test: At the start sprint to the left or right, then to the other cone, then proceed to sprint back to the start.

10. T-Test: At the start sprint to the left or right, then to the other cone, then proceed to sprint back to the start. Then backpedal 5 yards, at the cone sprint forward through to the start.

11. Vertical figure 8: Run a vertical figure-eight around 5 cones with 3 yards in between each.

12. W-Drill: Start with 8 cones 5 yards apart at a 45 degree angle, forward and backward

13. 3-Box Drill: Place 3 boxes (or make squares with cones) on the 5, 10 and 15-yard lines. Keeping your hips facing in the direction you are running, get around each box as fast as possible, then sprint to the next box. After the last box sprint to the 25 yard line.

Coaching Cues:

Do each drill properly and quickly. Maximum effort equals maximum results.

Coach:

Bruiser Flint is the head coach of the UMass Basketball program at Massachusetts, taking over the reins when John Calipari left to take over the NBA New Jersey Nets. The Minutemen compete in the Atlantic-Ten Conference.

Off-Season Strength and Conditioning
January '97 NABC Courtside

Purpose:

Provide a self-monitored off-season conditioning program for all basketball players.

Description:

In the past decade, basketball has undergone an evolution of sorts. Players are much bigger, stronger, and quicker. At the root of these characteristics are weight training and conditioning programs. Implementing a solid, well-developed program is imperative if you want to build a successful basketball program. Failure to do so is, in effect, accepting mediocrity.

As coaches, it is essential that we get our athletes to understand that weight training and hard work in the offseason directly affect their success during the basketball season. Many coaches do not have the benefit of strength and conditioning coaches, so we ourselves must become knowledgeable of this very important aspect of college basketball.

The overall goal of the off-season strength and conditioning program outlined here is to produce physical gains relative to success on the basketball court. The program should be structured so athletes are challenged, but not so demanding that they give up on parts of the workout. A maximum of one hour per day dedicated to strength and conditioning is not too much to ask. Getting through the first two to three weeks is the key; once athletes begin to see and feel the tremendous gains this program produces, it will be hard to keep them away.

The program is set up on a five-day cycle. During each cycle, every major body part will be worked out once, cardiovascular work will be done, as well as "basketball" conditioning. It looks like this:

Day 1: Chest and Shoulders
Day 2: Back, Triceps & Cardiovascular
Day 3: Legs and Biceps
Day 4: Conditioning
Day 5: Off

The Weight Program

A weight program is probably the most vital aspect for basketball players in the off-season. To neglect the weights is to accept the fact that you're just going to fall behind other players who will dedicate themselves. Weight training during each five-day cycle should be alternated between so-called heavy workouts (more weight, fewer repetitions) and light workouts (less weight, more repetitions).

On heavy days, we work with five to eight repetitions. This is where players make their greatest strength gains. On light days, we work to get 9 to 12 reps with each set. This is where players achieve muscular endurance. Application of both of these principles is important as basketball playing utilizes both muscular strength and endurance. Each workout should take no longer than one hour. If it does, then players are resting too long between sets. Two minutes between each set should be sufficient before the muscles are ready to be worked once again.

Sets should be performed pyramid-style. The first set of each body part (not the first set of each exercise, as those muscles are already warm) should be a warm-up set of approximately 15 repetitions, then "pyramided" by increasing the weight and decreasing the reps until the last set is the heaviest. If the athlete gets below his target reps, decrease the weight so the player gets back to the desired rep range.

All exercises should be done for 3-4 sets. Athletes should monitor on paper all work done to ensure proper evaluation and to see the gains made and goals accomplished.

Proper execution and technique for all lifts is very important as bad form can cause injury and other undesirable effects. Players should use the proper breathing techniques, go through the full range of motion during each rep and not cheat by using momentum or other non-targeted body parts. It should also be noted that the use of a spotter is very important, so players can go for that last rep and be assisted on the positive phase of lifting.

Day One

Chest (do 1 and 2, and 3 or 4): Alternate which one of the first two done first each workout:
1. Flat bench press
2. Incline bench press
3. Dumbbell flies (flat or low incline)
4. Wide-grip dips (lean in at bottom of movement to isolate chest)

Shoulders (choose 3):
1. Military press (behind-the-neck)
2. Dumbbell press
3. Dumbbell lateral raises
4. Dumbbell frontal raises
5. Close-grip rows

Day Two

Back (choose 3):
1. Pull-ups
2. Lat pull-downs (to the front or back)
3. Seated cable rows

4. Bent-over one arm dumbbell rows

Triceps (choose 3):

1. Lying tricep extensions
2. Close-grip bench press
3. Cable push-downs
4. Weighted dips (hands and feet on two separate benches with weight on lap)

Cardiovascular: Choose any cardiovascular machine (stair-master, treadmill, etc.) and perform at between 70-85 percent of maximum heart rate for at least 30 minutes.

Day Three

Legs (do all 4):

1. Squats
2. Leg extensions
3. Leg curls
4. Calf raises (sets of 30 reps)

Biceps (choose 3):

1. Barbell curls
2. Alternate dumbbell curls (seated or standing)
3. Seated incline dumbbell curls (simultaneous)
4. Concentration dumbbell curls

Day Four

Conditioning: This conditioning program should take no longer than 35 minutes for each workout. It is aimed at improving quickness, agility, muscular power (explosiveness) and cardiovascular fitness. It's important to warm up before beginning the workout. Five minutes of light jogging followed by two minutes of light stretching will be sufficient. All conditioning should be done with 100 percent intensity.

Begin the workout with five minutes of rope-jumping. Jump on both feet for two minutes, then on the right foot only for one minute, followed by the left foot for one minute, and again on both feet for a total of five minutes. After a one-minute rest, move on to rim touches with both hands (the backboard, or a high spot on the wall can also be used). As soon as the feet return to the floor, explode back up without hesitation using the arms for momentum, both hands reaching full length above shoulders. Repeat for 30 seconds, rest for 30 seconds, and repeat again. After completing the second set, rest for one minute.

Up next are plyometrics. Using either two stairs or a 1½-foot bench. The first exercise is to continually hop up and down with both feet for one minute. Rest one minute, then go on to one foot at a time. Step up with the right, up with the left, down with the right, down with the left. Go for one minute. After another minute's rest, do the same, except lead with the left foot. Again, rest one minute and then do hops with both feet for another minute. Rest two minutes upon completion of plyometrics.

The quick-feet drill is next. This drill greatly improves agility and is especially good for big men. Each component of the drill should be done continuously, with no rest between exercises. Set up the pattern shown here on the floor and do the exercises described below (see Figure A).

Diagram 84-A

1. Up and back
   a. Place feet on points A and B.
   b. Jump to C with both feet
   c. Jump and place feet on points D and E.
   d. Without turning, repeat the process backwards.

Repeat the cycle for 10 up-and-backs.

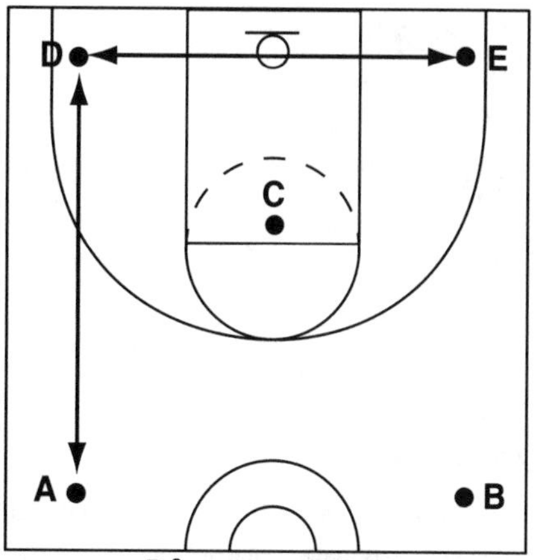

2. Right Foot
   a. Start on B and jump to C on the right foot only.
   b. Go to D, E, C, A, and B in that order and repeat for 10 times around.

3. Left Foot
   a. Follow the same pattern as for the right foot for 10 times around.

4. Both feet
   a. Follow the same pattern as for one foot (as if skiing) for 10 times around.

At the conclusion of the quick-feet drill, players should have conditioned for about 25 minutes, provided the pace indicated throughout this workout was maintained. Athletes should now cool down with a 2-3 minute walk. Don't just stop and sit down!

The last 8-10 minutes is a stretching period. Stretching is done lightly before the workout for warm-up, and afterwards, while the muscles are warm, to increase flexibility, reduce soreness, and aid in recovery.

This off-season program is very demanding; however, each weight workout takes less than an hour and each conditioning workout takes no longer than 35 minutes, and the effects that it will produce should not be underestimated.

If your players follow this program faithfully, they will become bigger, stronger, quicker, and better basketball players. You will find that this program will contribute greatly to your team's success for next season. All it takes is a little time on your part to implement it.

Coaching Cues:

Challenge athletes and set up a recording/monitoring system so each player can measure their status and follow their progress.

Coach:

Ben Drake is an assistant coach at SUNY Brockport, an NCAA III school.

DRILL

85

Plyometrics Conditioning

Purpose:

Teach players a method of basketball conditioning to prevent injuries and increase muscular power to improve basketball performance.

Description/Coaching Cues:

Would you start a player who has never been on a running program to begin by running a marathon? The obvious answer is "no." Would you start a player who has not been on an explosive jumping program begin by jumping off a 39" box and to jump back up? I hope the answer is no again – but a lot of coaches who do not understand Plyometrics begin at a level too difficult and end up creating problems. Plyometrics, like any adjunct program, needs to be started at an appropriate level and developed over an appropriated time scale.

The program we have been using – Muskingum starts slowly with Thermetrics (warm-up Plyo's) then goes to Blyometrics (Basketball Specific Activities) then to Plyometrics (actual jumping, leaping, and bounding activities).

Where to start and when to start each level depends (just as it would if you started a weight program) with an understanding of the individual involved.

The chart in Figure A shows the program broken down into three separate sections. The idea of developing power from speed and strength is not new but can be helpful to your program. The number one benefit we have seen at Muskingum is in the area of injury prevention and reduction. The program has been set up and put into action by the Muskingum College Men's Basketball Program. Both the coaching staff and the players believe it has been a very good program for the developing of power and explosiveness in the athletes.

Coach:

Jim Burson has been head coach of Muskingum College for 30 years. He has won over 436 games, which places him 1st in all-time Ohio Athletic Conference wins. He helped with the selection of the Olympic teams in 1984 and 1988. He was recently named to the Board of Directors of the NABC.

DRILL
86

Off-Season Basketball

Purpose:

Teach players to structure off-season play so as to create guidelines that produce realistic competition.

Description:

Almost every coach realizes the importance of out of season development by his players. Our coaching staff continually stresses that everyone improves during the regular season and that the only way to get ahead of your competition is by determined work during the so called "off" season. The coach must impress on his players that there is no such thing as an "off" season for the truly dedicated athlete.

Many fine programs have been started for individual development of players. Quickness and reaction, ballhandling, weight training, and conditioning programs are available and used in many schools. No matter what their individual development program involves, players always find time to actually play the game and many times this is where bad playing habits are acquired. At Lipscomb University, we have given our players basic rules that have helped them to eliminate bad habits and play the kind of basketball that has improved their basic skills during "off" season play.

We encourage our players to use the following games and guidelines when they play during the "off" season. All games reward the ball possession back to the scoring team. This make-it/take-it policy rewards good offensive execution and emphasizes aggressive defense in order to gain possession of the ball.

Four-on-Four

We prefer four on four as our basic half-court game as it is much more realistic in terms of offensive and defensive game action The weakside is occupied offensively and the help side is filled defensively. This eliminates the unrealistic, easy backdoor basket that three on three and two-on-two permit.

Game Administration

1. Teams receive one point a basket. They play to eleven and must win by two baskets.
2. The ball must be passed in from the top of the circle to start play.
3. Everything is to be cleared to the top of the circle before the team gaining possession can attack the basket.
4. The offensive team and the defensive team both call fouls that occur.

5. Players must try to work on eliminating the silly foul such as reaching in on defense.

Playing Rules

1. After a player gains possession, he is allowed only two dribbles. A third dribble is a violation which results in loss of possession. This rule curbs overdribbling and selfishness, promotes team play and passing, and creates a desire among offensive players to move without the ball. Guards quickly learn to move to the fast break outlet spots after their bigger teammates get the defensive rebound.

2. The offensive team must make at least four passes before shooting unless they can get a layup or get the ball into the post area before the fourth pass. This rule teaches our players to look inside and promotes unselfish team basketball.

3. The offensive players are to pass and screen for a teammate away from or pass and cut to the basket. We want these two types of movement as they fit into our basic offensive philosophy.

4. When an offensive team passes into the post area, they are to react to the defense and move accordingly.

Cutthroat

Our players use this game to improve their quickness and reaction. It can be used as a nine player three on three game or a twelve player four-on-four game. It is excellent in that more players are involved at each basket. The emphasis on quick transition, movement on and off the floor, and quick starting of the offense teaches players to hustle without a coach constantly yelling at them.

Game Administration

1. There is one offensive team, one defensive team, and one ready team waiting out of bounds on the baseline. Each team wears a different color jersey.

2. Teams receive one point a basket. They play to eleven and must win by two baskets.

3. The ready team calls all fouls and violations.

4. The offensive team must start the ball at the top of the circle and fill the two wing positions before passing the ball in to start play.

5. The team which scores should immediately hustle the ball to the top of the circle and begin play immediately.

6. The defensive team scored upon quickly leaves the floor and becomes the next ready team.

7. The ready team that was waiting must hustle to the defense since the offense will not wait for them.

Playing Rules

Our players use the same playing rules as described for four on four.

Three-on-Three

We use the same game administration and playing rules as listed for four-on-four. We only encourage three-on-three when there are not enough players for four-on-four.

One-on-one

We have adopted the following rules for one-on-one in order to make these games more realistic and complementary to our team style of offense.

Game Administration

1. The game is scored the same as a regulation game. The two players play to eleven and must win by four points.
2. The offensive player works from various spots on the floor.
3. The game starts when the defensive player crosses a line fifteen feet from the basket.
4. When the defensive player captures the rebound, he hands the ball to his opponent and receives it back after he assumes an offensive position.
5. Both the offensive and the defensive player call any fouls.
6. If a player makes a one shot foul, he keeps possession of the ball. On two shot fouls, the second shot will determine possession. We believe that shooting all fouls has helped eliminate excessive fouling and created pressure free throw shooting situations.

Playing Rules

1. There is a three-dribble limitation placed on each possession of the ball. A fourth dribble results in a violation and loss of possession.
2. If a player cannot beat his opponent for a good shot, he must give up possession of the ball. A forced shot is a violation and results in loss of possession.

Full-Court Games

We do not encourage full-court play as we want more people to play a longer period of time. Half-court play also allows more work on basic skills, emphasizes passing, encourages defense, and creates a team situation during "off " season workouts. Players always seem to want to play full court and when they do we ask that they play in the following manner.

Game Administration

1. Teams receive one point a basket. They play to eleven and must win by two baskets.
2. All full-court games are four-on-four or five-on-five.
3. We use the make-it/take-it rule. If team A scores at basket A, they will take the ball out of the basket and attack basket B. Team B remains on defense until they stop team A from scoring. We have found that most players do not want to play as much full-court basketball when they find that there will be no trading of baskets in order to gain possession of the ball for their one-on-one dribble move.

Playing Rules

1. Our players are instructed to always look for the fast break.
2. Once the offense crosses half court they are limited to two dribbles a player after each possession of the ball. This creates the passing and movement that we want in our team offense.

3. If the offensive team does not get the fast break layup, they must make four passes before they shoot unless they can get a layup or or hit the post area before the fourth pass.

When players are not involved in one of the games described above we encourage them to shoot free throws, perform ballhandling drills, or work on individual offensive moves. We constantly remind our captains to urge members of the squad, to thank teammates for passes, screens, and defensive help and to encourage aggressive play. This will carry over into the game schedule and will promote greater team cohesion.

Coaching Cues:

Simulate game competition and create guidelines that reward team play.

Coach:

Don Meyer, head coach at Lipscomb University in Nashville, TN, is one of the winningest active college coaches at any level of play. A native of Nebraska, Dr. Meyer's teams are noted for their fundamental skills, up tempo play, and team focus. His teams are a fixture in the NAIA I Top 20 rankings, having won the national championship in 1986.

3-on-3 Halfcourt/Half to Full/Fullcourt

Purpose:

Teach players all offensive and defensive skills in a competitive situation.

Description:

This drill begins in the frontcourt at the halfcourt line with six players at a time, three on offense and three on defense.

All offensive and defensive situations should be practiced: 1-on-1 moves (outside/inside), plus 2-on-2 situations (pass and cut, pass and screen – away from/to ball, pass and replace self). Players can rotate from offense to defense to off the court substitutes.

After proficiency is attained, the drill progresses from halfcourt to an O/D transition to a fullcourt basis on made or missed baskets. Finally, six players at a time play 3-on-3 fullcourt, offensively and defensively. Offensive players can be restricted to dribbling the ball, not passing over halfcourt.

Basketball Hall of Famer Ralph Miller felt that the 3-on-3 fullcourt drill is the most important fundamental skill drill in basketball – it can expose players to all offensive and defensive situations that can be encountered.

Coaching Cues:

Focus on all offensive and defensive skills and principles – it is especially valuable in teaching man-to-man pressure defense and effective offensive play against pressure.

Coach:

Ralph Miller was elected to the Hall of Fame in 1988 after a storied playing and coaching career. He garnered Coach-of-the-Year honors in three major conferences – Missouri Valley, Big 10, and Pac 10. In 1981 and 1982 he was national Coach of the Year. Miller played and learned his "pressure basketball" concepts, emphasis on fundamentals under the first basketball coach, Hall of Famer "Phog" Allen of the University of Kansas.

DRILL

88

60-Point Game

Purpose:

Teaches players a "feel for the game" and offensive motion offense principles – spacing, moving without the ball, passing-catching, and playing against pressure defense. Defensively, the drill teaches pass denial, "dead ball" situations (offensive player with the ball has used the dribble).

Description:

The offensive/defensive game is played on the halfcourt; 3-on-3, 4-on-4, or 5-on-5 with no dribble allowed. First team to 60 points is the winner; 1 point for pass, 5 points for score, extra point for designated move (back-cut score, screen resulting in score, etc.). Possession changes on turnovers or missed shots. Coach may allow layups only, or any type of designated score.

Coaching Cues:

Offense – emphasize basic principles of passing - catching, 15-18 ft. spacing, moving without the ball, setting and using screens, catching - facing basket - protecting ball, offensive rebounding.

Defense – pressure ball, deny all leads off the ball, pressure shots, block out and defensive rebound.

Coach:

Dan Monson became the head coach at Gonzaga University (WA) following nine years as an assistant with the Bulldogs. He is assisted by Mark Few and Bill Grier. GU teams have been in postseason play for the past three years, topped by their first ever NCAA I postseason bid in 1995 when the head coach was Dan Fitzgerald.

Pressure 2-on-2

Purpose:

Teach offensive players to get a good shot in a short period of time and defenders to prevent easy scores, blockout and prevent second shots/secure the ball.

Description:

Coach starts drill by offensive players running a preselected offensive option (pick-and-roll, pass and cut, backdoor, etc.) in a 2-on-2 situation with 9 seconds left on the clock (start clock when pass to offensive player is caught). This drill creates some bad shots so is excellent to work on blockout/rebounding.

Coaching Cues:

Offense – no wasted motion, execute effectively and quickly. Get a good shot.

Defense – anticipate, take away strengths, no easy shots, blockout – contact, go to ball, capture ball with both hands, chin the ball (may outlet to coach).

Coach:

Jerry Krause, NABC Research Committee Chair, has been coaching for 33 years.

Diagram 89-A

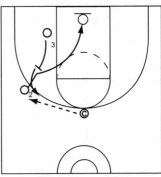

Diagram 89-B

Fast Break Breakdown

(2-on-0 to 1-on-1, 3-on-0 to 2-on-1)

Purpose:

Teach two lane and three lane fast break passing, fast break 2-on-1 defense, and fullcourt 1-on-1 for offense and defense.

Description:

2-on-0 to 1-on-1. 1 and 2 start 3 ft. outside the FT lane and pass 2-on-0 fullcourt to score at the other end. Shooter becomes defender going the other way; other player grabs ball out of net to become offensive 1-on-1 player (see Figure A)

3-on-0 to 2-on-1. Three players either go straight down court or use 3-man weave to score at other basket. The shorter sprints to defense and defends against a 2-on-1 situation, as seen in Figure B.

Coaching Cues:

2-on-0 to 1-on-1.
Offense – get ahead of the ball, pass where the man will be.
Defense – contain the ball, turn the dribbler, take away dribbling strength.
3 on 0 weave to 2-on-1.
Offense – pass and cut behind receiver to sprint up court, pass where man will be.
Defense – force the extra pass, buy time for teammates, prevent the layup.

Coach:

Frank Carbajal is head coach at Hartnell College in Salinas (CA). This highly respected coach has been coaching 35 years.

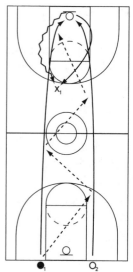

Diagram 90-A

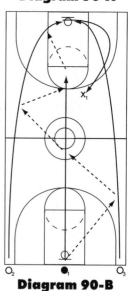

Diagram 90-B

DRILL 91

3-on-2, 2-on-1
Fast Break Drill

Purpose:

Teach players offensive and defensive skills in primary (outnumbered) fast break situations.

Description:

Coach passes the ball to a baseline offensive player (Figure A). The defender at that position must sprint to touch near baseline before going to transition defense. The three baseline players fast break on a 3-on-2 situation (Figure B). The player that scores becomes the defensive player in a 2-on-1 fast break at the opposite basket with the two defenders becoming offensive players (Figure C).

Coaching Cues:

Offense – get the ball to a ballhandling guard. Run lanes 2 feet from sideline (3-lane break). Read the defense and make sure point guard stops at FT line. On the 2-on-1 fast break, split the floor and read driving and passing lanes.

Defense – versus the 3-on-2, back man takes first pass, high man drops to protect basket, communicate with the third defender. On the 2-on-1 – fake and retreat, stop the layup, take the ball away from best ballhandler.

Coach:

The head coach of Yale University, Dick Kuchen has 30 years experience. He has coached at University of St. Louis (MO), Notre Dame, Iowa and California.

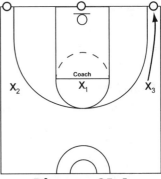

Diagram 91-A

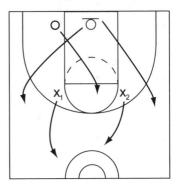

Diagram 91-B

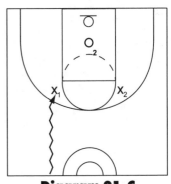

Diagram 91-C

3-on-2 Fast Break Continuity Drill

Purpose:

Teach players offensive and defensive fast break skills and strategies plus fullcourt conditioning.

Description:

Drill starts with three players at one end of the full court creating a rebound from the backboard, outletting the ball and filling the three lane fast break.

As depicted in Figure A, three A's attack B_1 and B_2. When last A crosses 10 sec. line, B_3 runs to center circle, steps inside and becomes third defensive player. A's exit to right (defensive players always exit to right).

After A scores or on rebound, B's take ball out or outlet the ball and go 3-on-2 against A's at opposite end. A_6 is trailer defender, (A's) press to midcourt line (see Figure B).

In Figure C, drill continues –with defense and offense rotating.

Coaching Cues:

Offensive emphasis is placed on ballhandling at top speed under control. The offense must get a good shot quickly as the trailing defender quickly makes the 3-on-2 fast break advantage into a 3-on-3 situation. Run the drill for 12 minutes and keep statistics on shots, rebounds, and errors.

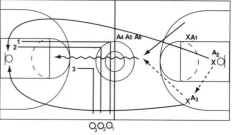

Diagram 92-A

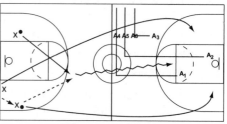

Diagram 92-B

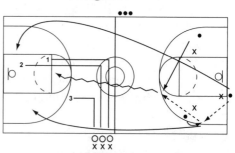

Diagram 92-C

Coach:

Denny Crum has coached at Louisville since 1971 and directed his 1980 and 1986 teams to the NCAA I Championship. Denny played and coached at UCLA under John Wooden. His teams are noted for their up-tempo style of play. He is also on the NABC Board of Directors.

DRILL 93

Continuous 4-on-2 Fast Break Drill

Purpose:

Teach players offensive and defensive execution of the primary three lane fast break in a 4-on-2 situation and fullcourt conditioning.

Description:

The drill starts with basic 4-on-2 from midline. Two additional defenders join first two defenders after all offensive players cross halfcourt line. All defenders touch center circle before going to defense – first 2 when opponents get ball possession. Three different colored shirts needed for three teams (or light/dark reversibles and skins). The drill is usually run 10 minutes and score can be kept.

Four white shirts break versus two dark shirts. W_1 drives to the right elbow, W_2 and W_4 (wings) angle cut from side and v-cut back out to 3 pt. Trailer W_3 goes to left elbow then cuts to right block. Any op-

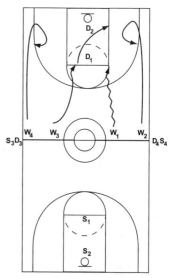

Diagram 93-A

tion for quick shot (W_1, W_2, W_3, W_4) and offensive rebound. D_3 and D_4 run in and touch center circle after all four offense players cross center line then join in on defense. After steal, defense rebound, or score. The four dark shirts form break and attack two defense skins at other end, and the process repeats. Skins 3 and 4 join 1 and 2 after four offense players cross midline.

Coaching Cues:

Need 12 players to use this drill – three teams of four players. If more than 12 players on the squad, use them as substitutes to join their team at midline. Form break properly on offense – get a quick shot (3 passes maximum). Coaches need to officiate. Defenders must communicate and hustle.

Coach:

Dean Nicholson is head coach at Yakima Valley College (1995 to present), after coaching at Central Washington University from 1964-90. He also coached at Puyallup (WA) High School from 1950-64. He and his father coached over 50 years at Central Washington. His teams won numerous NAIA District Championships. Dean has been inducted into the NAIA Hall of Fame.

Combination Drills   **185**

Fast Break Recognition Drill

Purpose:

To teach players to recognize whether to run a primary or secondary fast break in an offensive situation with an offensive and defensive team.

Description:

This is a fullcourt combination drill using all players on the squad (14 is assumed in this situation).

The squad is divided into a defensive team of 7 players who are positioned out-of-bounds near the halfcourt line. The coach with them numbers them 1 to 7. When play begins the coach randomly calls from 1 to 5 players by number to initiate defense. The defenders must get one foot inside the halfcourt circle before they retreat to play defense. For example, if coach calls #4 and #2, those two defenders sprint to the center circle and then defend the offensive team coming down the court. The defensive coach can then release three other defenders to help on defense (touch center circle, communicate, and find open offensive players).

The other players start underneath a basket in a defensive situation (Figure A) and their coach with a ball. Five players at a time begin the drill in defensive rebounding spots (5, 4, and 3 under the basket; 2 in the key; and the point guard 1 blocking out the shooter, who is the coach). These five players get the rebound or take the ball out-of-bounds to start the fast break.

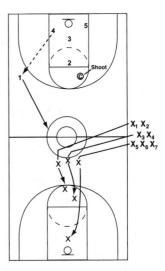

Diagram 94-A

Coaching Cues:

If there are two or less defenders, the offense runs a primary three lane fast break with the ball in the middle lane, as shown in Figure B. If there are three or more defensive players back in the first wave, the offensive team takes the ball to the sideline and runs the secondary fast break (Figure C). The first big man down the floor (4 or 5) sprints to the low post block on ball side.

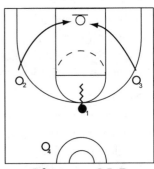

Diagram 94-B

The offensive team can run any of the secondary fast break options. They then transition from offense to defense.

Coach:

Coach Roy Williams heads the legendary Kansas University program, where the first basketball coach, Phog Allen, coached. Coach Williams has maintained the famous tradition, having won conference or tournament championships and garnering national coach-of-the-year honors. He was a former assistant to Dean Smith at North Carolina and presently serves on the NABC Board of Directors.

Diagram 94-C

4-on-4 Change

Purpose:

Teach players to think and react quickly and change quickly from defense to offense and vice-versa – transition.

Description:

Begin play 4-on-4 on the halfcourt, as shown in Figure A. 4-on-4 with an extra ball with passing coach (C_2). The drill can be used to focus on offensive or defensive strategies until the primary coach (C_1) calls "change" – this signals a reversal of O to D and D to O for the two teams, as the player with ball (O_2) instantly places the ball on the floor and sprints to defense. Coach (C_2) passes the new ball in play to anyone on the X team (now on offense) as a manager retrieves the ball left on floor and passes to C_2 to get ready for the next transition.

Coach C_2 may allow the teams to go back-and-forth a few possessions before again calling a "change."

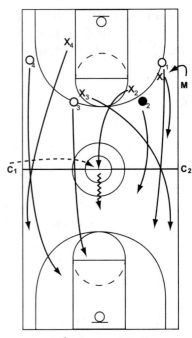

Diagram 95-A

Coaching Cues:

Be alert – think and move quickly. Communicate on offense and defense – sprint from offense to defense. Move with control from defense to offense.

Coach:

Phil Martelli took his 1997 St. Joseph's (PA) to the Atlantic-10 Championship and to the NCAA I Sweet Sixteen. His two years at St. Joe's were 45-20 and his 1996 team went to the finals of the NIT.

Northwestern Switch Drill

Purpose:

Teach players the team skill of instant transition and the individual skill of thinking quick.

Description:

Switch and Change

Switch – Half Court Transition (see Figure A)

On the coach's command of "switch":

Diagram 96-A

1. The offense (O_1, O_2, etc.) switches to defense.
2. The ballhandler, O_2, should place the ball at his feet.
3. The defense (X_1, X_2, etc.) switches to offense.
4. Do not switch ends of the court.
5. The new defensive players, the O's must now defend the same basket they were just shooting at.
6. The O's cannot guard the opponent that was just guarding them.
7. The new offensive team, the X's, tries to score immediately.

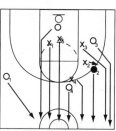

Diagram 96-B

Change – Full Court Transition (see Figure B)

On the coach's command of "change":

1. The offense, the O's, sprints back on defense to defend their goal.
2. The ballhandler places the ball at his feet.
3. The O's can defend any of the X's in transition.
4. The X's can attack the O's to score immediately.
5. The O's must point and talk their way throughout the transition.
6. Play continues as the coach designates.

Coaching Cues:

The coach controlling the switch/change calls should make the calls on an ir-regular pattern so that players cannot anticipate the calls. <u>Focus</u> on defensive com-munication and transition skills.

Coach:

Kevin O'Neill, the head coach at Northwestern University (IL), also completed successful stints at Marquette University and the University of Tennessee.

Combination Drills   **189**

Team Transition
(4-on-4, 3-on-3)

Purpose:

Teach players effective O to D transition skills and teach offensive players to convert to offense quickly.

Description:

The drill begins with four lines on the baseline (teams of 4) with the first defensive transition group at the free throw line extended (see Figure A). Four offensive players are on the baseline. The coach begins the drill by passing to any one of the baseline offensive players. The opposite defender at the FT line must touch the baseline before making the transition to defense while all other teammates sprint to defense immediately.

The offensive group fills the lanes and attacks the defense in a 4 on 3 situation. The three defenders must protect the basket, stop the ball and cover offensive players until trailing defender recovers. At this end of the court, play continues until the defense makes the stop (steal or defensive rebound) or the offense makes a basket – then the offense sprints back to the opposite FT line extended and defenders go to the end of the line on opposite baseline.

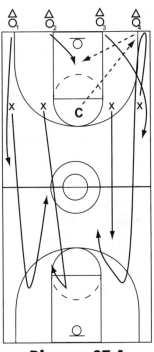

Diagram 97-A

Coaching Cues:

Defense – sprint back with vision, protect the basket, stop the ball, communicate, buy time for your teammate.

Offense – get the ball to a ballhandler, push ball up the floor by pass or dribble, make good decisions, and get a shot for the best shooters.

Coach:

Rusty Smith, presently an assistant coach at University of California, Riverside, has been coaching 14 years, after playing at Montana State and professionally in Europe.

Arizona Team
Defensive and Transition

Purpose:

Teach players team defensive concepts in a sequential, progressive form.

Description:

4-on-4 or 5-on-5 defensive drills – depending on whether team consists of 12 or 15 players.

3 times and out. This halfcourt drill version focuses on defensive effectiveness. The team on defense must stay on defense until the offense has been stopped three consecutive times. Count fouls as made baskets to discourage the defense from "hammering" an offensive player in the basket area. Coaches make corrections during and between possessions. Additions for emphasis can include: offensive rebounds counted as a made basket, offense required to make a certain number of passes before the shot, or offense required to get a shot for a certain player.

3 times out with transition. The team on defense will fastbreak from a missed shot. If the score is on the fast break possession (break or pre-set offense), they receive credit for two of the required three "stops" on defense. This version forces the offense to keep defensive balance and make O to D transition to stop the offensive thrust. It also helps the defense work on outlet passes, filling their fastbreak lanes and flowing into pre-set offense positions.

Up and back. In this form, we focus on O to D transition and vice-versa. The group on offense will start with the ball at halfcourt. They make a pre-designated call of their defense to play on the made or missed shot. The team on defense alternates zone and man defenses so the offense has to recognize and practice against both types of defenses.

The offensive group attacks the defense then converts to defense. We utilize this drill to work on press offenses and defenses. The drill can be varied by starting with a free throw situation or continuing full court until one team scores six points. One advantage of this drill is that it allows us to dictate defensive situations and give team feedback/corrections to both teams immediately after each performance.

Coaching Cues:

O to D transition – get a good shot, rebound or get back on D, sprint to defense, talk, cover the basket and all players.

D to O transition – prevent easy scores, blockout and get the ball, top speed under control, read the defense, find the open man, get a good shot.

Coach:

Legendary Lute Olson capped a 24-year coaching career (535-200) with a NCAA I National Championship in 1997 for the University of Arizona. His 14 year Wildcat record is 343-108, including an amazing home court winning streak of 71 games. He is also the University of Iowa's winningest coach. At Arizona, his teams have been to three Final Fours, seven PAC-10 titles, 13 consecutive NCAA I Tournament appearances and the nation's best winning percentage over the past 10 seasons.

DRILL 99

Team Transition 5-on-3

Purpose:

To teach players team timing of skeleton offense, made basket fast break (primary or secondary), offense entry and options against three defenders, and O to D transition.

Description:

Realizing that most coaching staffs are pressed for time and are looking for combination types of drills, I'd like to give you our five-on-three drill. Initial Alignment is shown in Figure A.

First, we have the five offensive players dummy through an offensive series based on the

Diagram 99-A

coach's call, score the basket (we never let them stop until they do), take the ball out of bounds and fast-break against the three defensive players at the other end.

Once they get to the other end, they try to score off the break. If this is not successful, they get into early entry until they score or the defense gets the ball on a rebound or turnover.

As soon as the defense gets the ball, the two players who have been standing on the side of the court near the 28-foot line, step on the court and the five defensive players now attack the other end. They can throw the long pass, if the offense does not make the transition back to defense. They run the break and go into early entry if the break is not successful and we have a five-on-five situation.

Once the defensive team scores or turns the ball over, we end the possession and start all over. We do not change teams until we have run all of our offensive series.

Should we have more than ten players, we will either have the extra ones shoot free throws on the side until they make ten – then rotate into the drill, or we may have an assistant carry on another drill with them and rotate drill participants. If you are coaching alone, the extra players can be on the side spots of the three-team.

If you have enough coaches, it may be best to put one at each end of the court. We tell the "3" end to run whatever the "5" end does in dummy. With only one

Combination Drills   **193**

coach, we position him at mid-court and give instructions to both groups. You may wish to shorten positions of the players on the side if they are starting to "cherry pick."

We find this drill to really be a time saver. The "5's" learn to run motion, run the break, get into early entry, must make the transition, and play defense. The "3's" play passing lanes, outlet the ball, run the break, get into early entry, and play 5-on-5.

As well as a teaching aid, the drill serves as an excellent physical and mental conditioner, involves a lot of people and allows a lot of coaching to take place.

Coaching Cues:

Coaches can focus on the whole team of five or the three defenders. Any team offensive option may be used.

Coach:

Pete Mathiesen was head coach for many years at Chico State University (CA) where his teams were consistently successful. He now teaches at Chico and works with youth to prevent violence and combat gang behavior.

DRILL
100

4-on-4-on-4

Purpose:

Teach players transition scoring, movement, getting open without the ball and man-to-man defense.

Description:

Start with one team of four players in light uniforms (or skins), one team of four players in dark uniforms (or shirts), and one team of four players in pinnies. Place a team at each end of the court and put one team at mid court with the ball. Team with the ball plays against one of the other two teams. Play as normal (with coaches officiating) with emphasis on helping others to get open (through screens off ball or two man game with the ball). On turnovers (violations, offensive fouls, out of bounds) or defensive stops (steals or defensive rebounds), ball goes to defensive team, who then goes in transition fast break to the other end of the court against the third team. On made baskets, ball goes to whichever team gets the ball out of the basket first, and that team goes on the break. Once a team has the ball in transition, the team that just lost the ball cannot steal the ball and must stay at the basket that they are at and wait for play to come back to them. The new defensive team then picks up the man-to-man at half court. Once the ball crosses half court, the defense is free to steal the ball. Team with most baskets at the end of session (it is best to play for 15-20 minutes) wins.

Coaching Cues:

As stated earlier, the key aspect of this drill is working to get each other open. You can work on two man game as well as moving and cutting away from the ball. With only four men on offense, this opens up the middle considerably. Other points include emphasis on staying wide on wings during transition (spreading out the defense) and filling the lanes on the break.

Coach:

Entering his 20th season as head coach at Southern Connecticut State University, Art Leary is coming off his program's best season ever in 1997, as his team posted a 28-4 record and in the process the Owls won their first ever New England Collegiate Conference championship, and made their first appearance in the NCAA II Elite Eight. Leary was an assistant coach at Quinnipiac College for seven years. A 1970 graduate of Quinnipiac College, Leary holds a Masters Degree in Education from SCSU. He is also a member of the NABC Research Committee.

444

Purpose:

Developing up-tempo pressing and fast break style of play.

Description:

Figure A shows three teams of four – Black (B), White (W), and Red (R). Red runs numbered break against Black toward north basket. B_1 and B_2 are in tandem. As soon as ball crosses half court, B_3 and B_4 sprint to center circle and then back for help defense. Play until field goal is made or defensive rebound. Change of possession on a steal or turnover.

In Figure B, after change of possession by a steal or turnover, Black runs numbered break against White towards south basket. W_1 and W_2 are in tandem. As soon as ball crosses half court, W_3 and W_4 sprint to center circle and then back for help defense. At the same time two Reds set up at Black basket in tandem. One Red goes to midcourt side A; one Red goes to midcourt side B.

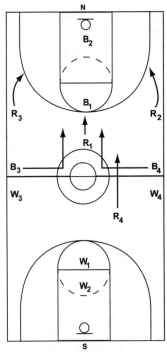

Diagram 101-A

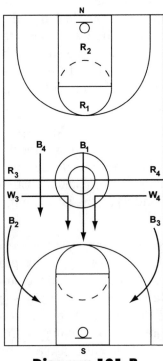

Diagram 101-B

Coaching Cues:

The "444" drill is introduced as a fast break drill, but is eventually developed into a pressing drill. In other words, after a made field goal or "dead" ball, the press is on until the ball crosses half court. When the ball crosses half court, the drill is consistent with 444 Fast break. You can run any type of four-man press. The four players who get in the press after scoring learn to get to the correct spots quickly.

Coach:

Orlando "Tubby" Smith is the 20th coach in Kentucky University history to head their men's basketball program. Prior to leading the Wildcats, he was a UK assistant for two years with Rick Pitino, spent four seasons as Tulsa Golden Hurricane head coach and two years with the Georgia Bulldogs. His uptempo style of play is known as "Tubbyball" – fast breaking, pressure defense, and three-point shooting. In addition, Coach Smith has extensive experience as an assistant college coach and head high school coach.

DRILL
102

Four-on-Three Drill
February '97 NABC Courtside

Purpose:

Teach players to scramble in an outnumbered defensive situation; guard the ball first, protect the basket, and help your teammates. Offensive players learn to shoot under pressure while both groups learn rebounding skills.

Description:

Four-on-three Contest the Shot is one of mainstay drills here at the University of Georgia. It incorporates many skills and techniques on offense and defense. It first teaches the three defenders to quickly take the open man with the ball, because they are at a disadvantage. Guarding the ball is our No. 1 priority. When taking the ball, players must call "ball" loudly. Communication is important.

Secondly, we are teaching the defense to close out, to contest the shot without fouling and to box out. We "high jump" and do not "broad jump."

Third, it teaches our offensive players shot preparation, how to use shot fakes and pass fakes, how to recognize open shots and to go to the offensive boards.

Diagram 102-A

Diagram 102-B

The procedure of the drill is simple. A coach passes the ball to any offensive player to start the drill (See Figures A and B). The offense has five passes to shoot and must stay stationary except for a shot fake and one dribble. On the shot, all players rebound.

The defense must rebound a missed shot on two consecutive plays to complete their defensive turn. If there is no contest or no box out, their successful tries goes back to zero. If the "open" man rebounds (there are four on offense and three on defense) that turn does not count and there is no penalty.

This drill is a very intense drill. We often use it at the end of our defensive segment before water and free throws. Because it incorporates transition, man-to-man defense, offense, and rebounding, it is one of our most valuable and versatile drills.

Coaching Cues:

Players must contest the shot, box out, and rebound two consecutive times to rotate. If offense player who is not boxed out rebounds, "open man" is called and drill is started again with no penalty.

Coach:

Ron Jirsa is head coach of the Georgia Bulldogs, who are noted for their pressure defense and up-tempo play. They have been to NCAA post-season play on a regular basis.